Study of a case in psychogenealogy

Reflections on Transgenerational Trauma

Claude-Alain Saby

Study of a case in psychogenealogy

Example of a family from Auvergne

ISBN : 978-0-244-49239-7

A few words from the author

This book is the translation of the book :
"Etude d'un cas en psychogénéalogie",
ISBN 978-1-326-79650-1
This book is available for free reading on Calameo at
https://www.calameo.com/read/002960208376d68bfc9cb
and available in paper format at http://www.lulu.com

Many readers have asked the author for an English version of this book.

The author has done this task but asks for the indulgence of the readers because the English language is not his original language so that many errors of vocabulary or syntax may have spread throughout the pages of this book.
Thank you for not being too strict.

The author will be pleased to receive your comments at the following address: patronymesaby@gmail.com

This study is part of a larger research project

Table of Contents

Foreword

"I can't grasp everything I am"
Augustin d'Hippone

In the first half of the 17th century René Descartes (philosopher) already suspected that if the individual experience of the world was stored in memory, not all memory was accessible to the consciousness. In the 19th century, the psychologist Hermann Ebbinghaus wrote in La Mémoire that most experiences remain hidden from consciousness, but nevertheless produce significant effects that authenticate their past manifestations.

Thus we could say that our activities, our thoughts, our beliefs are the final products of activities of our memory and our nerve cells if we refer to the work done in recent years in neuroscience. To simplify, we inherit a certain genetic construction plan and are born in an environment that leaves us no choice throughout the most important years of our training. Equality between Men is therefore a decoy, if not a myth, a collective fantasy.

Our inner space is immense, hidden, intimate but nevertheless we can try to get to know a small part of ourselves simply by questioning our ancestors, it already implies getting to know them. The dead, even forgotten and unknown, can be very talkative and influential.

From a scientific point of view, we do not control our behaviour, we are dependent on our genes and their particularities, each one is built from a genetic plan. The conscious mind is not the captain of the ship. The rudder is held by the unconscious brain, itself formatted by life experiences and instinctive programs produced by previous generations.

The brain produces our behaviours in very complex ways, reflecting the fact that people cannot be equal. This variability is the driving force behind evolution because people's genetic profiles and personal histories shape their brains and thus mark their differences.

This is why people end up having very different worldviews, different personalities and no less diverse decision-making capacities[15].

The machinery that makes us the people we are is not simple. Neither biology nor the environment alone can shape our personality. We are the result of a sum of too complicated equations; the case study, in this document, will attempt to provide some insights through the analysis of several generations of the same family.

Galileo's discovery ejected man from the centre of the Universe, but by falling from his pedestal, human beings gained a better understanding of themselves, exploring their inner cosmos as if to answer Michel de Montaigne's questions as early as 1571 with his question "who am I?" or the sentence written on the pediment of the Temple of Apollo in Delphi "Know thyself". We are complex beings with hundreds of millions of neurons, peripheral nervous systems, "zombie" processes, complex activity patterns as well as the biology and chemistry of our brain.

Thus our mental life is largely influenced by a long list of factors from diverse and more or less accessible backgrounds. Our health is confronted with the onslaught of diseases that seem to result from many minor changes in our DNA, which occur simultaneously and according to interaction patterns that are as complex as they are dependent on interactions with the environment. This is how it is easy to understand that psychological stress can exist when an individual moves from one group to another, or from one region or country to another. This stress is all the greater if the host population shows a low degree of acceptance. This social exclusion can take different forms, such as a greater sensitivity to diseases, depression, anxiety, various disorders such as schizophrenic stress. But not everyone reacts in the same way to this question, for various reasons such as the fact that there are genes that predispose to depression, to violence, to name but a few. Whatever the notion of belonging or not to a group is very important if we want to explain certain psychological imbalances of individuals.

These few lines were necessary to say that our ancestors are not responsible for all our ills. But it is important to keep the bond that unites us with them.

Important decisions in our lives can be influenced by insignificant details such as the choice of a first name, a covenant by assonance that is not necessarily the result of chance. Dates of birth, a place, can experience a feeling of benevolence in us, whereas it is generally the manifestation, quite often, of an implicit egotism, that is, the magnetic power of unconscious love that people carry to themselves, which has the effect of influencing their judgments.

Let us keep this aspect in mind when we study the repetition of life scenarios.

In a novel the characters are projections of parts of us, but in the story of a genealogy it is the characters who constitute us by sketches, simple or more complex features. We are part of a set of heterogeneous inherited figures. We are the result of a huge patchwork of which we know little.

A family tree is the perception of a vertical world that is visualized on a sheet of paper filled with signs, transforming this still life into animated matter. We're exploring the field of our memory.

Holding your family tree in the palm of your hand is like holding on for a while, ours. Time has become matter. Building your family tree is like taking a walk in an immaterial world, you bring nothing with you, you walk freely, you observe without judging, you come back empty-handed but you don't come back unscathed. Our unconscious has long been colonized, but now the results of this colonization are coming in to make their voices heard.

A few more words....

In the turmoil of the past harassed by the present,
our family tree does its duty of intelligence.

Our collective memory has taken a turn for the worse and is in danger of sinking. We recall wrongly, we distort the memory, we reject history according to the manifestations of minorities.

For short-sighted political reasons, the country is losing its memory and jeopardizing its future.

The preservation of shared memories is disturbing; yet they are the result of a human construction that began a very long time ago.

Collective memory is not only the sum of individual memories, but also requires that there be points of contact between them and that there be a strong cement recognized by all.

The risk is to be taken in hand by a present without inheritance and a future without a project. Whose fault is that? To minority pressure groups and inconsistent and cowardly policies that have been tearing apart our history, our memory, our conscience for several decades.

We live in an age of stealth image, circumstantial emotion, and zapping.

Family trees are damaged because they disturb certain current ideologies. The Church and the administrations since the 14th century have worked well. The archives in France are numerous and well kept. They have withstood years, wars, revolutions, weather conditions.

These archives are valuable. They are a wealth of information to understand the past and to understand us.

In addition to surnames, first names, dates, a more detailed analysis opens a new dimension to the understanding of our personal history.

The answer to the question "who are we?" is there before our eyes. Statistics, psychoanalysis, psychogenealogy, social psychology, help us to understand the life of our ancestors, their difficulties, their joys, their torments, the causes of their traumas, and the transgenerational propagation of them.

To know your past is to build your future. But it is more than that in reality because we are not witnesses or victims of the past, but we are the main actors.

Studying your family tree means finding ruins, reviving people, making them talk and helping us to progress.

Our individual memory is a ghost ship that must not dismast at all or risk damaging our Unconscious Mind.

The rural pages of our past are despised, probably voluntarily.

Rurality is reduced to its reassuring, friendly, bucolic aspect. These clichés mask the harsher, appalling realities of people paralysed by hunger and submission.

The "indigenous peasants" were taken out of their "reserves" in 1914 to save France's honour, without specifying and worrying that the vast majority were sick.

A million and a half deaths later and names on marble, we pretend not to see the traumas of the soldiers who came back as well as the traumas of young widows and children who did not or little know their father.

Women are singularly absent in history.

The peasant memory, too disturbing, does not interest people in the cities. Modernity will take charge of giving the final blow to a campaign immobilized by repeated misfortunes.

The tyranny of the present time has settled easily. We do commemorations, places of memory, we place plaques in memory of...

But this bric-a-brac (odds and ends) of stories doesn't make history.

History and memory are opposed, they are "at right angles", Peguy[1] would have said.

Psychogenealogy may be one of the unifying features between historians so often and unjustly indicted and the bearers of outraged memories, self-proclaimed victims who want to impose their own reading and exclusive vision of history.

Psychogenealogy, does not lie, it goes back in time, talks about people, listens to the dead. She studies those who are no longer in their geographical and social environments.

Thus, in the turmoil of the past, harassed by an ideological, selfish and devastating present, the family tree quietly does its "duty of intelligence".

This book, through the example of an Auvergne (*) family, will try to bring it out of its opacity.

(*) Auvergne is a region in the centre of France with ancient volcanoe)

---

1   Charles Peguy, writer, (1873-1914)

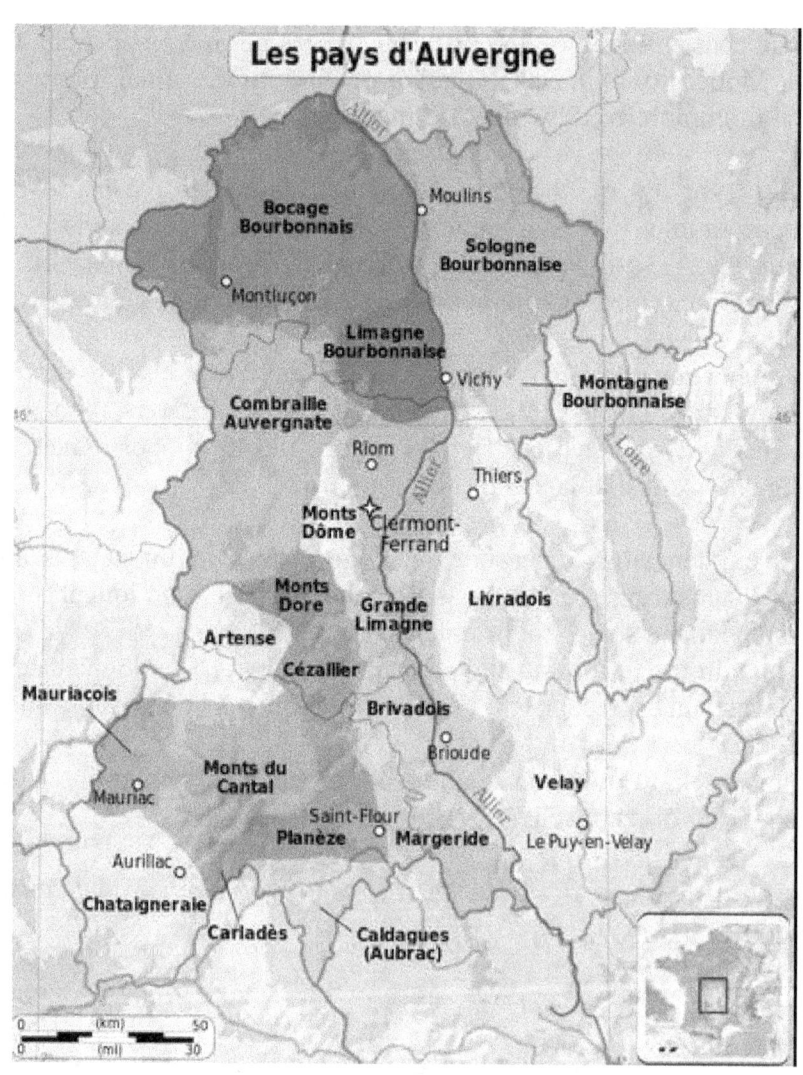

Les pays d'Auvergne

Chapter 1

Psychogenealogy
Some important reminders

The coincidences observed in family trees can be simply due to -chance. But they are more likely than we think a priori.

-In her book "Aie, mes aieux ! ", Anne Ancelin Schützenberger [5] [6], delivers, through her clinical analysis and professional practice of nearly twenty years, a therapeutic study on transgenerational traumas in psychogenealogy.

We would, she said, be a link in the complex and ramified chain of generations and we respond (or suffer) to the facts of life of our forefathers.

A life without history does not exist.

So we all have problems. But we all also have a personality that consists of repeating behaviours, words, emotions, thoughts. Do these acts belong to us? This is not certain and certainly not all, because we are a reflection of psychological types that predate our birth. We are not the masters of our game, but we have the illusory feeling of being an independent character. Each of us can find ourselves trapped in a scenario that we have not built. It is a kind of "invisible loyalty" that pushes us to repeat, without being aware of it, without wanting to, pleasant situations or painful events. We are less free than we think to be what we would like to be; our personality itself is built on personal systems of interpretation that result from education and the surrounding culture. However, we have the opportunity to regain our freedom and get out of the repetitive fate of our history, by understanding the complex bonds that have been forged in our family.

Some life scenarios over generations are ephemeral but others are repeated, more or less constant: there are generations of girl mothers, orphans, violent men, people who live long or short lives for example. Our life scenario is imposed on us in the debate but we will have to find our "happy end" by ourselves and leave behind modified scenarios, with or without mitigated effects, with unpredictable and unexpected consequences.
We start our lives with a quota of information and a quota of amnesia so that we can think about our lives and give them meaning.

The craze for genealogy has given rise to a new discipline that has become almost indivisible: psychogenealogy. Anne Ancelin Schützenberger[2], claims the creation, about thirty years ago, of this neologism, combining the two terms: genealogy and psychology.

Her theory is based on observations she has made during her career, psychogenealogy can be defined as a method of psychoanalysis which consists in searching in the experiences of our ancestors the sources of our possible psychological disorders, strange behaviours and/or current diseases. Anne Ancelin Schützenberger synthesized the results of her observations and developed her psychogenealogical theory in her book "Ow, my ancestors! "« Aïe, mes aïeux ! ».
Psychogenealogy is based on different concepts of psychoanalysis, including that of the collective unconscious developed at the beginning of the 20th century by Sigmund Freud's disciple, Carl Gustav Jung, but also the concept of invisible family loyalty and that of "ghost".

---

2 Anne Ancelin Schützenberger, psychotherapist, analyst-group and psychodramatist, professor emeritus at the University of Nice where she directed the laboratory of social and clinical psychology for about twenty years

For C. Jung[16][17][18], the collective unconscious is the set of images and motifs that symbolize the fundamental instincts of Man. It manifests itself in the form of archetypes, i. e. ancient images, which are found in myths and legends, and which would be common to all humanity. These archetypes would manifest themselves in dreams, delusions and certain forms of art.

Jung distinguishes several levels in the collective unconscious: first the family collective unconscious, then the ethnic and cultural group collective unconscious and finally, the primordial collective unconscious (where we find everything that is common to humanity such as the fear of darkness, the instinct of survival).

Pierre Daco[19] presents a diagram reproducing the psychoanalytical conception; we see a character rowing on the surface of a lake that could be compared to the conscious individual, that is, synthesizing his various perceptions (the three-dimensional space in our allegory),

"Suppose this rower has never dived or had the opportunity to know that this lake has a bottom. He therefore believes that nothing exists below him, and therefore that there is nothing other than his conscious life. »

He will assume that there is something when he sees a bubble burst on the surface; so there is an invisible part that is probably very large and very complex called Unconscious[3].

Thus the bottom of the lake represents the "it" « ça » (subconscious). From time to time this bottom releases bubbles (symptoms) that burst the surface of consciousness and prevent some things from happening at the bottom. If these bubbles are powerful, they may upset the boat and we will talk about neurosis.

The unconscious and the subconscious act through nerve centres.

---

3 Aware that unconscious facts may become conscious as needs arise

The Unconscious is a word that resonates in the current discourse. But this word engages a charge of ambiguity since it is a kind of active psychic fiction that doubles reality[4], a reality that exists outside us.

The unconscious is the most popular word in psychoanalytic theory, the most fundamental concept of the problem opened by Freud more than a century ago. This hypothesis of the Unconscious is thus necessary because of the inconsistencies of conscious life.

By placing the unconscious at the heart of his system, Freud thus rethought the separation between the conscious and the unconscious, gave it more rationality by developing a dynamic of processes.

Jean-Paul Sartre (philosopher) never admitted the reality of the Freudian unconscious, this catch-all instance of the repressed, he said. "How can I believe in a thought in me that is not a thought of me? For Sartre, the unconscious is simply the result and the name of a consciousness that refuses to be consciousness. Thus, during an analysis, he does not become aware but aware of what he was already aware of, his hidden complex. Disagreement about unconsciousness arises from disagreement about consciousness.

Freud sees consciousness as a function of discernment and control, while in Sartre consciousness is choice, intentionality and existence.

In Freud as in Sartre, man deludes himself and gets lost, he is mistaken about himself and himself. Dreaming, hysteria, hallucination are deceptions. But for Freud, "it" -ça- deceives the "me"-moi-, while for Sartre, consciousness is lying herself.

For Alain the unconscious is a misunderstanding of the "me"-moi- and that, to make the unconscious a buried and tyrannical identity is a fault.

In his Cahiers, Paul Valérie contests less the reality of the unconscious than the conditions of its establishment and transmission.

Unlike Sartre, Maurice Merleau-Ponty admits the reality of the unconscious but deeply discusses its nature.

---

4   "psychological reality" according to Freud

The philosopher Paul Ricoeur[5] offers an original analysis of Freud's work. He argues that the unconscious does not think, that it exists only as a diagnosed reality, constituted by a work of interpretation in the context of the psychoanalytic cure. Ricoeur thus sketches a confrontation between phenomenology[6] and psychoanalysis.

There are still many works such as those by Ludwig Binjwanger, Medard Boss, Heidegger, Adolf Grunbaum, Karl Popper and many others, which will not be mentioned in this document.

Carl Jung[7] therefore has, as mentioned, an interesting approach by proposing two unconscious ones.

Jung[8] distinguishes "a layer which is almost superficial from the unconscious", which he calls "personal unconscious", and a "deeper layer which does not come from personal experiences or acquisitions, but which is innate". "This unconscious has contents and modes of behaviour that are the same everywhere and in all individuals. In other words, it is identical to itself in all men and constitutes a universal psychic foundation of a supra-personal nature present in everyone". Jung explains that he chose the term "collective" to emphasize the universal nature of this deep layer of the unconscious. While the contents of the personal unconscious are "complexes with an affective tone, that form the personal intimacy of the psychic life"..., "the contents of the collective unconscious are the archetypes".

This term, writes Jung, "tells us that we are dealing, in the collective unconscious contents, with old[9] or, preferably, original types,

---

5 *De l'interprétation*, essai sur Freud, id Seuil 1965
6 Edmund Husserl, fondateur de la phénoménologie
7 Carl Gustav Jung est un médecin, psychiatre, psychologue et essayiste suisse né le 26 juillet 1875 à Kesswil, canton de Thurgovie, et mort le 6 juin 1961 à Küsnacht, canton de Zurich, en Suisse alémanique (source Wikipedia)
8 Dans son étude intitulée *Des archétypes de l'inconscient collectif* (publiée pour la première fois dans les *Annales d'Eranos*, 1934, et reprise dans *Les Racines de la conscience*, Livre I)
9 le grec "arkhaios" signifie "ancien"

which means universal images that have always been present". He immediately clarifies that "the notion of archetype is only indirectly suitable for collective representations", as found in myth and tale, "because it refers only to psychological contents that have not been subjected to conscious elaboration". He therefore reserves here the designation of archetype to "a psychic data which is still immediate", such as it arises in dreams and visions and which is "much more individual, more incomprehensible or more naïve than, for example, in myth". Then, considering that this immediate psychic data is "an unconscious content modified by becoming conscious and perceived, and this in the sense of the individual consciousness in which it emerges", he finally establishes, in the note relating to this passage that" one must, to be exact, distinguish between "archetype" and "archetypical representation".

The archetype itself is a hypothetical, non-manifest model, such as the biologists' "pattern of behaviour" (the above paragraph has been borrowed, the source is not known or has not been found).

Thus C. Jung speaks[10] of archetypes as virtual images: "The form and nature of the world in which the "being" is born and grows are innate and prefigured in him in the form of virtual images". Thus parents, women, children, birth and death are innate in him in the form of pre-existing psychological availability, in the form of virtual images, which "are like the sediment of all the experiences lived by the ancestral lineage; they are the structural residue, not the experiences themselves".

Jung talks about the archetype of the father, the archetype of the mother, the archetypes of the anima (imprint and image of the feminine in men) and the animus (imprint and image of the masculine in women), as well as the archetype of the Self -Soi- that governs the individuation process. But it also speaks of the archetype of the divine child, of birth, of the divine couple, of the old wise man, of unity, of the tree, of the cross, etc. One can be tempted to speak of archetype about each of these images, so rich and profound is the meaning of each one.

---

10 Dans *Dialectique du moi et de l'inconscient*

There would then be a multiplicity of archetypes.

Jung points out that this collective unconscious implies a certain heredity. However, in Psychology of the Unconscious (1913), he writes: "I do not affirm in any way the hereditary transmission of representations, but only the hereditary transmission of the capacity to evoke this or that element of the representative heritage". This idea was later taken up by Jacob Lévi Moreno[11] who developed it and postulated the existence of a co-inconscious family or group that would be the vector of a transgenerational transmission.

As early as 1913, in Totem and Taboo, Freud wrote: "We postulate the existence of a collective soul (âme) and the possibility that a feeling would be transmitted from generation to generation relating to a fault of which men are no longer aware and have the slightest memory. "evoking the possibility of transmission by an unconscious person connecting members of the same family.

Invisible family loyalty[12] is the second important concept in psychogenealogy. This invisible family loyalty is intimately linked to the concept of family justice. Within a family, everyone maintains a subjective accounting of what they have given and received in the past and present and what they will give and receive in the future. There would be unconscious rules of loyalty and an unconscious accounting system in each family that determine the place and role of each member and their family obligations, including respect and propriety.

Anne Ancelin Schützenberger talks about the Family Accounts Ledger.

For her, the discharge of family debts is very often transgenerational: "What we have received from our parents, we give back to our children. "Concretely, she says, this implies that someone

---

11 Jacob Lévi Moreno 18 mai 1889- 14 mai 1974, il est un des pionniers de la psychothérapie de groupe
12 développé par Ivan Boszormenyi-Nagy, un psychanalyste d'origine hongroise qui publie en 1973 avec G.M. Spark : Invisible loyalties

who has had a childhood that is too spoiled compared to his or her brothers and sisters, who has not respected his or her family's moral code - for example, by denouncing one of the members or committing a crime - risks carrying an unconscious debt and passing it on to his or her descendants over several generations.

These rules of loyalty are called invisible because for psychogenealogists, they are unconscious.

To illustrate this concept of invisible loyalty, we can cite these theoretical examples very often cited: "a child fails the baccalaureate unconsciously in order not to exceed the social status of his parents, a girl takes charge of the education of her siblings when her parents die and never gets married, a niece takes care of her old aunt because she saved her father's life during their childhood".

Invisible loyalty rules would therefore sometimes keep people in servitude. They would feel bound by an eternal gratitude for services rendered. These rules can give rise to resentments, resentments that are themselves passed down from generation to generation. Inheritance matters are a perfect illustration of this, with the frustration they create.

The transgenalogy[13] is thus the consideration of everything that affects us at the level of the body, the soul, the spirit from our ancestry.

Our ancestors therefore take such an important place that it is important to know them, to analyze them, to see what they have done right or wrong without seeking to thank them or accuse them.

For Jodorowski our family tree is carried and its knowledge can, through work in the mind, in the flesh and in the spirit, allow us to expel demons. First of all, we must know how to place ourselves within this tree; we are not alone, we are linked to others to the living and the dead.

The family unconscious does exist with its traumatic unspoken words. But if we are burdened by it, we are also responsible for the future of our descendants. Our responsibility is enormous. The path is full of all kinds of abuse: material, sexual, emotional, relational; drawing up an exhaustive list would be long, but at most it is possible to prioritize the facts. Some people do not want to die so they express themselves through subtle contortions, but they will emerge one day in the course of an event.

A majestic tree can produce bitter fruits, a modest tree can produce good fruits. What ultimately matters is the trauma experienced and above all felt.

Trauma is our inner temperature. It is this temperature that he makes us aware of.

Our ancestors also leave us a space in the measure, for example, that we estimate our life expectancy according to those known in our tree, we plan the stages of our life by keeping in mind what our ancestors did as the ages of marriages, births. "Some suffering is natural, we value it because it is part of a family tradition. The dream of perfection within oneself cannot exist because perfection has no universal definition.

Our ancestors are therefore alive, more or less active, our ancestors meddle in our destiny sometimes so strongly that they can

---

13 Alexandro Jodorowski

prevent us from living our personal script forcing us to reproduce a past scenario. The relationships that our forefathers had are also alive and relevant; so we can make friends or enemies both alive and dead. They influence our actions as we manipulate them to serve a cause. The past interferes in our dreams and the unconscious momentarily becomes surreal.

According to Françoise Dolto[14], the Bible is, moreover, and above all, a work of transgenerational theories that have nothing to envy to current theories.

We are not marionettes (puppets) because through subliminal, subconscious attention, we find all kinds of information, mostly harmless; this attention allows us to interpret them and act.

This information is the pieces of a puzzle whose final image we will never have, but it allows us to chart our course while directing our personal consciousness by putting it, or not, in harmony with the clan consciousness of a family in the broad sense.

Each of us is caught in a family bubble, wrapped in some kind of invisible waves that embrace us more or less strongly. The settling of scores between generations is prohibited, only awareness, changes in trajectories and corrections are tolerated. Forgiveness (pardon) is not allowed because it would imply that there is a presumed guilty party and also a judge.

The chronological order could only be a set of signals with oscillations, harmonics, changes in slope, trajectories, ruptures that we would have to unravel (or unscramble).

The concept of "ghost[15]" has been ignored by Freud while Chinese Taoists measure one fate over nine generations and the Bible over three or four.

A "ghost" is transmitted from generation to generation.

---

14 « L'Evangile au risque de la psychanalyse »
15 Concept élaboré par Nicolas Abraham et Maria Torok

Murder or suicide, incest, bankruptcy, adultery, children out of wedlock, homosexuality, paedophilia, sex, mental illness... it is rare that a family's history does not include any of these episodes, perhaps even more so in our time than until the middle of the 19th century when "situations" were more stable, governed by prohibitions, codes that were both simpler and more rigid.

They are delicate topics of conversation, undefendable, and are rarely mentioned by family members. But these secrets, which we often keep silent out of shame or simply to avoid cluttering our lives with undesirable and disruptive elements, can become real ghosts for psychogenealogists.

This transgenerational aspect had in fact disappeared from all Western thought for more than one or two centuries, while Chinese, Amerindian and African thoughts are receptive to this mode of human functioning. Taoism cares about the dead, about those who are "evil dead" and who in one way or another continue to haunt us. To worry about these deaths is a work of mental hygiene because we are haunted by all those of us who died without having been able to solve their biggest emotional and psychic problems.

Freudian psychoanalysis has ignored death in order to focus only on mourning. For Freud, the unconscious is made up only of the experiences forgotten since our childhood. For Nicolas Abraham, these forgotten experiences can concern our parents and more distant ascendants.

The transmission of trauma can have a collective dimension: the ghost of Auschwitz can bring back the exterminations of Protestants in the 17th century in the Cévennes, hunger in Africa can remind us of the famine of farmers in the 18th century, the exodus in Syria can remind us of the exodus of Auvergne at the end of the 19th century, or the exodus of the French from Algeria, the Spanish under Franco and many other cases.

The ghost is an emotional, family, cultural, social structure that we duplicate very early on, by building our mental structures into those of our parents. The ghost is therefore an object of the family structure.

For Françoise Dolto, for example, psychosis had to be reflected in three generations. The work of transmission is carried out in several stages according to her, first of all of an unconscious nature (psyche of the foetus or original mental activity).

The individual psyche is only formed around the age of three and until that moment the baby lives in a community psyche that is the one of his family. Thus a mechanism of psychic structuring is set in motion. A child does not learn to speak, he duplicates his parents' language as he duplicates their mental structures.

Nicolas Abraham and Maria Török invented the notions of crypt and ghosts. They imagine that a secret could have been locked by the unspoken in a crypt of the unconscious family and emerged to influence the behaviour of their patients. For Nicolas Abraham and Maria Török, a ghost is therefore a formation of the unconscious born of the unspoken secret of another member of the family and transmitted from one unconscious to another through the generations. For psychoanalysts, the secret and the unspoken, all the occult words act, "like invisible elves who manage to break from the unconscious the coherence of the psyche".

To summarize, psychogenealogy postulates the existence of a family unconscious allowing transmission between generations, the existence of rules specific to each family and the possibility for a traumatic past event[16] to influence the behaviour of family members. Many family secrets are healthy and legitimate, but others weigh very heavily on the psychological life of some people whether they become delinquents, drug addicts, enter a spiral of failure or fall ill. Overprotection of a child by his parents can damage his creative mind, non-communication can exclude him from a community and lead him to a certain physical and moral drift.

---

16 For the theorists of Freudian psychoanalysis, there is no such thing as a family secret

The essential tool of transgenerational therapy is the genosociogram (see Chapter 5). It is a family tree over five generations (or more), often made up of memory, supplemented with important elements of life (professions, places of residence, socio-economic context...) and dates of significant events (births, marriages, deaths, accidents, dismissal, illness...). The genosociogram may also include the habits of each member, whether professional, religious, dietary, cultural, sporting or other.

The genosociogram is therefore not an objective document. It is not limited to direct filiation, but we add all the people in our family who play an important role in our lives (uncles, aunts, nephews, cousins...). A few sign conventions[17] make it possible to materialize the gender of family members, agreements, people living together. In this graphical representation, we look for repetitions, dates, first names, professions, coincidences and then try to interpret them. This analysis leads to the study of the reasons for migration, changes in situations, changes in life expectancy, changes in the number of children, the effect of wars, changes in health status. Any change is important.

In our time, the definition of family has evolved somewhat. In the past, this definition was obvious, it was not questioned. We cultivated the memory of the ancestors, we gathered during vigils, religious holidays, at the end of the harvest. But this family was patriarchal and authoritative: let us nuance, however, given the late marriages, the early deaths, the marriages lasted little longer and the children were often orphans, at least in the countryside.

Today, this situation is being disrupted by new lifestyles, new forms of relationships between parents and children are emerging, a new form of organization is being put in place; families are increasingly being reunited, fragmented, complexified or single-parent families. Advances in medicine have led to the emergence of children with

---

17It is possible to adopt conventions of signs other than those mentioned

anonymous donors (in vitro fertilization). Children are raised with same-sex parents.

Morals are changing, some taboos are disappearing, such as those related to adulterous children, for example, and some feelings of shame are put into perspective. The same causes will not have the same effects because the social situation has changed in the same way as the evolution of society and morals.

The Internet provides children with new links, new "friends", ephemeral, virtual, misleading, exchanges become mirrors. Some of these exchanges are experienced in an intense way, modifying individual and family group behaviour, generating conflicts. If this horizontal axis represented by relationships becomes complex, the vertical axis represented by ascendants and genealogy remains because each human being has a filiation, i. e. a link, and each link has its history.

These two axes are essential to the psychological development of an individual with the fear of seeing the emergence of secrets of more and more families that could give rise to psychological damage over the following generations. Everyone has an unconscious knowledge of their family heritage. Fortunately all secrets, the unspoken are not toxic and fade over time depending on the severity and intensity of the emotional investment.

A genosociogram will give some priority to the domains revolving around origins and death and around what can taint a family's respectabilities (alcoholism, suicides, depression, madness,...), but changes (slope failure in signal processing) will be just as important to understand the evolution of a trauma after having sorted out the elements of interference.

However, individual destinies, each with its share of singularity, are not independent of the social field in which they appear and evolve. Social belonging, cultural and economic capital, modes of education, religion, aptitude for social and geographical mobility, historical conditions of birth and place of belonging of the family, all this will influence the future of individuals in a framework as broad as the mode of social integration, educational trajectory, occupation, emotional life but also on the physical aspect.

Concerning this last aspect, and if we simply consider the period corresponding to the end of the 19th century[18], the Auvergne farmers were smaller than the craftsmen (tradepeople) and people living in the cities. Their health was poor, suffering from lung and hearing problems and a poor general state of health, mainly due to difficulties encountered in feeding and consequently to food deficiencies.

Many were reformed when the call for military service was made. Despite this physical weakness they were all mobilized and fought in the First World War. It is in the army that these men discover a richer, more abundant and varied diet. If the education of the peasants was low, the men in the cities, better nourished, also received a better education. Teachers, professors, administrative, railway, postal and other personnel were, in general, exempt from military service.

During the First World War, people with a certain level of education were either exempted or sent to a regiment behind the fronts. This war introduced other changes, women emancipated themselves through work, peasants worked in weapons factories, many soldiers in the aftermath of the war settled in a region other than their region of origin.

The war has left enormous physical and psychological scars, the effects of which we are still suffering a century later.

The increase in the level of education has made people aware of the injustices related to their social position. The class struggle then became a reality. Class relations have become visible and social violence has passed through generations. As a result, society has become less rigid.

Parents now have a life project for their children that may include "succeeding", accessing another class while being concerned about respecting family tradition. This contradiction can lead to personal humiliation in the event of failure and lead the person to a dead end.

---

18 D'après les archives militaires sur les fiches de recrutement des départements du Puy de Dôme, de la Haute-Loire et de la Lozère

Children are now increasingly following different trajectories than their parents. In this way, we develop a double identity, the inherited identity, corresponding to our social origin and the expected identity, i.e. the place we wish to occupy.

Thus the role of each individual's "I"-Moi- is strengthened but it can become a burden if one does not know the inherited identity[19]; adopted children can develop phantasms that correct reality, fairy tales, which are mostly used to control adolescence, also often feature children seeking their origins[20][21].

Our social trajectory remains conditioned by a number of elements that are linked to our cultural heritage, if this capital fails at any level we will remain fragile. This is why it is difficult to skip social stages; people are more or less well prepared to occupy a social place to which they aspire. Any change in class, promotion or downgrading can be the source of neuroses[21], but this is not systematic.

The social lift is therefore very slow, if it exists. Not so long ago, joining the army was a backdoor way out of social condition; a break in the evolutionary process that allowed many to value themselves (we will remember Napoleon's officers, generals and marshals, almost all of whom came from the people, or even men who went to work land in Algeria, Africa and Asia, thus leaving their villages in Auvergne or elsewhere).

The child from a working class background encounters additional difficulties in that he is placed in front of an alternative, he is asked to access the upper classes, to become a bourgeois and on the other hand he is told that the so-called bourgeois are "bastards", an injunction dating back to the experiences of several generations of exploited people or feelings of being so. A law does not break or erase class

---

19 Boris Vian
20 Bruno Bettelheim : Psychanalyse des contes de fée
21 Freud

feelings and neuroses that can otherwise be repeated over several generations.

The family novel is nourished by social trajectories, by small and big secrets, by facts occulted voluntarily or not, by defects in transmission that can reappear, by resentments, shame, revenge, desire, fantasy, transgenerational disorders, genealogical impasses.
All this supplies the "unconscious family".

Working with terminally ill cancer patients, Anne Ancelin Schützenberger has identified in their genosociograms what she has called birthday or synchronous syndromes. By searching through her patients' family histories, she found repetitions of structure or age: cancer sometimes started on the birthday or at the age when a mother, grandfather or aunt had previously died of cancer or an accident.

For her, "the unconscious has a good memory. ».
This would explain why some people feel anxious or depressed every year at the same time without knowing why, or remembering that this is the anniversary period of the death of a family member, which they may not even have known. These repetitions or synchronies constitute the birthday syndrome.

In her book, Anne Ancelin refers to the statistical study carried out by Dr Joséphine Hilgard, published in 1961, which she believes confirms her intuition. This psychologist has reportedly shown that the onset of psychosis in adulthood may be related to the family repetition of a traumatic event.

Dr. Hilgard conducted a systematic study of the admissions to two Californian hospitals between 1954 and 1957, representing 8680 patients. By eliminating the records of patients over 50 years of age, and by making a first screening on pathologies (exclusion of alcoholism for example), she kept 2402 patients, 3/5 of whom were diagnosed with schizophrenia, 1/5 with manic depression, and 1/5 with psychoneurotics. Of these, only those whose first hospital admission occurred after marriage, the birth of a child and the death of a parent between the ages of 2 and 15 were selected for the study. Finally, there were only 184 patients left: 37 men and 147 women.

Josephine Hilgard noted coincidences between the age of the patient at the time of the parent's loss and the age of the eldest child at the time of the patient's first admission in 14 of the 65 women who had lost their mothers, and in 9 of the 82 women who had lost their fathers. In her opinion, these numbers seem sufficient for a statistical study and they demonstrate the reality of the anniversary syndrome (this conclusion is statistically controversial). As far as men are concerned, this correlation could not be made. Hilgard explains this by the fact that men would end up alcoholics more often (pathology excluded from the study) and women would be more prone to mental disorders. As scientific proof of the existence of the birthday syndrome, other psychogenealogists also mention the work of Dr Monique Bydlowski, psychiatrist, psychoanalyst and researcher at Inserm. She reportedly made similar observations by studying the birth dates at the Clamart maternity ward and then at the Port-Royal maternity ward in Paris.

In Nina Canault's book, "How do you pay for the faults of your ancestors? "Every day, I see birth dates or dates of conception that commemorate the death of a parent or grandfather or first child who has not been able to mourn. »

To develop her theory, Anne Ancelin Schützenberger relies on her observations and a library of more than 300 family trees. She has surely used the most flagrant cases to illustrate her book, which contains some very surprising examples. Here are some examples (the sources of these examples are not known, which explains why they are not referenced).

"At 39 years old, Charles has testicular cancer. He underwent a first operation, then relapsed with metastases to the lungs and refused chemotherapy treatment, he would die. While making her family tree, the psychogenealogist realizes that her father and grandfather were butchers like him. She concludes that Charles believes in the use of the

knife, therefore the scalpel, and that is why he accepted his first operation without any problem, according to her. She then notes that her grandfather also died at the age of thirty-nine, from a camel kick in the testicles.

To summarize, Charles is about to die at the same age as his grandfather from a sickness he contracted in the same location... If she takes the study a little further, she realizes that the family structure is repeating itself. The grandfather died at 39 leaving a 9-year-old son and Charles is about to do the same. For her, it is more than a coincidence, it is an invisible loyalty.

"Roger is a doctor. At 27, he had a car accident when he brought his 6-year-old son to school. After investigating his father and grandfather, Roger revealed a repetition of accidents that occurred at the same age. For Anne Ancelin Schützenberger, this kind of repetition over 4 generations calls into question the randomness and can only be explained by an invisible loyalty. In this case, there would be a heredity of accidents among the boys in this family at 6 years of age.

"For years, François has suffered from sore throats and Reynaud's syndrome, a poor blood circulation of the extremities of the limbs, which gives a sensation of permanent cold. Building his family tree for many months with the therapist, he goes back to the French Revolution. He then noticed that one of his forebears, who was also called François, had been guillotined on January 9, 1793, his birthday. After playing this historical episode in psychodrama, all his symptoms would have disappeared.

All observations and interpretations of genosociograms can and should be discussed.

If the reality of transgenerational transmission phenomena can be allowed, one may wonder how a ghost can come out of its crypt to haunt one of its descendants and how this transgenerational transmission is possible.

"Anne Ancelin Schützenberger concedes that at the moment, nothing we know from a psychological, physiological or neurological point of view makes it possible to understand how something can bother generations of the same family.

"She nevertheless believes that the progress of a new science, psychoneurobiology, which studies the links between the psyche and the body, will provide answers. However, other psychogenealogists are already talking about genetic or cellular memory and hypothesize that our experience could be contained in our genetic heritage and thus be transmitted to our descendants.

These principles and theory of psychogenealogy are based on his observations and there is no particular statistical basis. Moreover, Dr Hilgard's study is itself very questionable because it does not meet the statistical tests. There could be confusion between correlation, concomitance or pure chance.

There are indeed date repetitions in family trees. However, this phenomenon is not always the result of coincidence.

"Thus, the calculation of probabilities often takes our common sense into error. An event that may seem improbable enough to us not to be a coincidence may in fact be much less surprising than it seems.

The example used by Henri Broch in his book "Le paranormal" is interesting: what is the probability that in a group of 50 people taken at random two people were born on the same day? Our logic encourages us to balance 50 people and 365 days, and therefore evaluate this probability at 50 chances out of 365, which represents a probability of about 14%. It is actually 97%, in other words, there is a 97 out of 100 chance that this event will happen. A genosociogram with 5 generations includes at least 32 people if it is limited only to direct filiation. In addition, it can be assumed that at least 3 dates (birth, marriage, death) will be associated with each of them. The probability of finding coincidences is therefore not as low as one might imagine at first glance. ».

Very often we try to give meaning to what is a simple coincidence. However, the reasons for this approach are interesting to study.

And even if these birthday syndromes were not due to chance and there was a correlation between traumatic events suffered by an ancestor and their consequences on his descendants, it would not demonstrate causality. There is therefore a lot of investigative work to be done.

In conclusion, the logical error not to do would be to confuse causality and correlation[22]. "Thus, in the example above, finding a correlation between the age of death of a parent and the age of the eldest child at the time of first hospital admission does not allow us to conclude that one of the events involved the other.

"The supposed beneficial action of psychogenealogical therapy does not allow either to scientifically validate the hypotheses on which the theory is based". There may also be a lot of subjection or self subjection, even manipulation.

The example presented below will try to reinforce the theory put forward by Anne Ancelin without seeking to validate it.

---

22 Effet cigogne : la corrélation est définie comme un indice statistique qui précise le degré de liaison entre deux variables ; elle ne doit pas être confondue avec la causalité, rapport qui unit la cause à son effet.
Stork effect: correlation is defined as a statistical index that specifies the degree of linkage between two variables; it should not be confused with causality, the relationship that unites the cause with its effect.

Chapter 2

Study of a case

"The human is the product of a story in which he seeks to become the subject"
Vincent de Gauléjac[23]

One of the aims of this document is, from a genosociogram, to develop models (this term is inappropriate) in order to approach phenomena from a different scientific angle.

A genosociogram is a "general ledger", it is also a table, a matrix, where debts, merits, but also rules are recorded on each column. These are contextual with biases that change over time.

These rules are complex, they emerge from the unconscious and from the "invisible rules of loyalty"[24], those things that are done without thinking about them because they correspond to family habits, unless they adopt a contrary behaviour and thus initiate a break-up.

A genosociogram over several generations reports significant events, whether positive or negative, with the qualities and weaknesses of each of the tree's actors, while maintaining a certain amount of subjectivity in the assessment.

First names are the first indicators, they have long accompanied a family "mission", a change in habits can express a family or national event.

---

23 Professeur de psychosociologie à l'Université de Paris VII
24 Ivan Boszormenui-Nagy (1920-2007)

Birthday syndromes[25][3]" are also important factors in understanding. Are certain events repeated over several generations? We observe generations of orphans, mothers, adventurers... Some dates come up frequently, simple coincidences or not, the interpretation of these repetitions requires a lot of caution, one fact may hide another. Repeated events are often tragic events such as bereavements, but they can also be pleasant. It remains to be seen when this tension decreases and finally disappears.

Each of our ancestors lived in a different epoch, so it is important to know the local history, lifestyles of the time, social difficulties, political events, their level of education and understanding of the environment in which they lived, the importance of the religious fact.

Before the First World War, people in the countryside spoke a local or regional dialect; the evolution was sporadic. Material conditions, mentalities and political consciousness underwent a rapid and profound change, especially after 1914. But the pace of this evolution was different according to the social milieu of belonging.

The 20th century saw the emancipation of women, awareness of workers' conditions, and an increase in the level of education. The erasure of traditions did not occur at the same time on the national territory, the gap was important, cities and countryside did not evolve simultaneously, France was not one and indivisible as it is often said.

To do a genosociogram is above all to do a preliminary identification by going back in time, to note why and how people have migrated from their region, to determine if there have been changes in their social conditions.

The analysis of these factors is essential.

There are gaps and omissions in our family histories and testimonies are rare, so it is crucial to put people and events in context[26]. We must therefore look back in the past and try to situate ourselves in

---

25 Josephine Hilgard
26 Ce que l'on appelle la Psychohistoire

its norms, its prohibitions without a priori. Without repeating History, we must try to understand the context in which they evolved. The stories of authors such as Balzac or Zola are important because of their descriptive nature.

Forgiveness, reconciliation and forgetting are three notions to avoid, we must not turn the page but simply read and analyze the facts noted therein while avoiding that the "toxic elements" affect us in any way. This neutrality is not easy, however.

Each of us surrounds ourselves with what J.L. Morano calls a "social atom", i.e. an environment that is composed not only of the elements that make up our family but also of other people such as colleagues at work, in hobbies or sports, neighbours, political members, trade unions, associations, childhood friends, enemies. This atom can be enlarged in a second circle by animals that are familiar to us or that we prefer. A third circle could correspond to the plant world, the type of trees, flowers, vegetables that we prefer. All this is to describe who we are. Other circles can be defined revealing what matters to us such as music, painting. J,L,Morano did not think that our dreams and memories can reveal an important part of ourselves, as we will see in Chapter 10.

A family, even if unknown or disappeared, is perpetuated at least in us in the form of quality or pathology with no awareness on our part. Psychogenealogy helps to reunite with our ancestors and allows us to understand the problems that have existed and eventually to solve them. Most of our forebears have suffered from hunger, disease, cold, difficult working conditions, low life expectancy, few people reached the age of 60 only one or two centuries ago. And yet, in the 19th century, for example, some people passed the age of 90.

A genosociogram can provide new insights into their lives and ours. But to carry out a good analysis, it is necessary first to gather a mass of diverse information and to immerse oneself in elements that fall within the framework of what is called social psychology.

We must not dream of going back too far in time, although in France there are civil status archives which have been compiled since the 13th or 14th century. We have only surnames, first names, and some dates for these periods. The relationships between children and parents were not the same as in our time, education was reduced or non-existent; the foundations of all research became inoperative in psychogenealogy.

On the other hand, the fact that one is a boy or a girl, whether one is an elder, second or youngest, has had a very strong importance in psychogenealogy and in social trajectories.

A child is born with a collective unconscious and in addition it is invested with the sum of the phantasms of its parents, its grandparents, close people like uncles, aunts, but also with the State which counts on it to perpetuate a policy, to maintain a civilization.

The child is thus charged with taking care of lost dreams, building or restoring them, he is asked to broaden a horizon that his parents have seen. A child may inherit cumbersome repressed desires or be forced to take a road he or she does not want to follow.

The filiation can thus be intellectual, legal, merchant, manual, artisanal, military, civil servant and any change of corporation can be badly experienced by the family and conversely by the person concerned. Each parent also tries to relive his own story more or less unconsciously through his child, proof of an archaic narcissism.

The social model has changed, the elders who imposed their law, who claimed to know everything, find a role they should never have left, that of a link in a genealogical chain.

Grandparents are no longer the distant and austere figures of old totem poles, as they were in the centuries before us, so we must take into account this past situation in our analyses, especially as we structure our identity by identifying ourselves with these different family figures and the vision they had of the world and people.

Psychogenealogy has become above all a self-knowledge, a key to explain our personality and behaviours, for some it can also be a therapy.

Chapter 3

Example of an Auvergne family

The tree studied will begin with Antoine's birth in 1678.

This family occupied the Combrailles[27] region between Saint Priest des champs and Biollet, in Basse Auvergne. It is a family of Auvergne not very well off.

There are few "ghosts" or harmful elements to be observed, but this is not a definitive observation. What we can say is that they were well integrated into a system, we observe that there was not too much reluctance to conform to norms or to submit to laws, which does not mean that these reluctances were not repressed causing some psychological damage.

As far as this family tree is concerned (for this surname), they have mainly worked as farmers and masons. The latter trade also expresses the fact that there were many members who migrated for several months.

In the middle of the 19th century, several of the members of this family migrated permanently to Beaujolais (a wine region north of Lyon).

The language of this region was a local dialect; in the 1950s, all the elders still spoke dialect among themselves. J. Semonsous, in his book "pages of history" written in 1938, wrote that of the 32,167 young people who participated in the conscription draw for 6 years (1827-1832), it can be observed that: 1204 could only read, 7146 could read and write and 22534 could not read and write.

---

27 Le nom proviendrait du gaulois comboro qui veut dire soit "confluent" soit "obstacle". Les Combrailles sont traversées par la Sioule

For example, when Mathieu (1833-1898), who moved to Beaujeu (town of Beaujolais in the Rhône department) in the 1850s and 1855, could not write and probably could not read when he married Jeanne D in 1859 (according to the extract from the marriage certificate). Maybe he only spoke patois (dialect).

We observe in this tree, after analysis, surprising phenomena of repetitions. There are thus significant events and shock events: illness, accidents, early deaths, departures from far away. Some of these lives look like novels, rather black for some, for many.

Analysing the family tree will make it possible to understand these facts, these repetitions, these coincidences. However, it is difficult to update all these invisible threads.

A family tree is not just a thing of the past, it is alive and present within each of us. Freud evoked the unconscious, Jung the collective and individual unconscious. The family or historical unconscious[28] also exists and is transmitted with all its emotional charges.

A tree is not a rational matter, it is an extremely complex organic being with its blockages, its desires and whose study must be done in a completely different way than by pure reasoning because the internal relations of the tree are mysterious.

The tree thus drawn in two dimensions is cold and incomprehensible, yet if we imagine it in its spatial representation, we observe unsuspected facts, connections appear from certain manifestations, a large net is set up, or rather a vast family constellation.

This is the whole purpose of this chapter where each generation will be studied in its historical, economic and health context.

---

28 The unconscious is not only a part of the shadow but also a prodigious reservoir of creative energy

The general features

Gervais, Marien, Annet, Antoine are first names that have been part of the family culture for several generations in addition to the traditional first names Henri and Jean.

For women, the first names were more classical with Marie, Anne and Jeanne.

Gervais, Marien, Annet are very old and not very frequent first names.

- the name Gervais was first mentioned in the 4th and 5th centuries because of the cult of Saint Gervais, bishop of Milan. In the Combrailles region (region to the north of Auvergne), where this family lives, there is a village called Saint Gervais d'Auvergne, the domain of the Counts of Auvergne in the 12th century, crossed by a Roman road that connected Augusto-Nemetum (Clermont to Evaux).

- Marien (from the Latin Marianus) comes from the name of a Roman family, Marius. He is seen as a masculinization of Mary.

- Annet is the English translation of Annette (Anne)

- Antoine has a Latin origin and was mainly carried to the 16th and 17th centuries.

- The name of this family probably comes from a Roman (Latin) name, this family comes from the Celtic people "Arvernes".

The settlement of this family on this land is ancient, there is a Roman influence and the probable influence of the Germanic peoples "barbaric invasions between 400 and 800, Cimbres, Sueves, Visigoths, Burgundians, Franks, Vikings), and perhaps English during the Hundred Years War (13th and 14th centuries).

There is little documentation on the countryside of the Lower Auvergne during the Upper Middle Ages. It was only from the 9th century onwards that the cartulars of Saint-Julien de Brioude and Saint-Pierre de Sauxillanges Abbey provided more extensive documentation, but their use was delicate, as the pieces were not dated.

At that time, probably as a result of population growth, men infiltrated the regions beyond the Allier plains. During the Merovingian period, thirteen agglomerations were certainly called vicus (villages). The vici located on or near the main roads have parish functions with churches, monasteries, priories, abbeys.

After the vici, come the agricultural establishments themselves. Sidoine Apollinaire and Grégoire de Tours report the existence of large rural domains, the survival of the large Gallo-Roman domains, divided, according to a classical scheme, into reserves and tenures united to the reserve by close economic ties.

Between the 9th and 11th centuries, the most abundant documents used various terms to describe these farms. So the terms: curtis, casa, villa.

The curtis (courtyard) groups farm buildings, community buildings, mills, a church, all enclosed by a fence.

The house would be the mansion, the master's house with courtyard, gardens, sometimes ploughed land, all also inscribed in an enclosure. The texts designate the curtis by the name of its owner, so there are several hamlets of the name of this family in this region. The peasant farms themselves appear under various terms, colonges, manses, appendaries, courtils, aises, ouches.

The manse and appendix are peasant farms for the use of a family.

In Auvergne, at the end of the 9th century, under the probable effect of a demographic boom, the "tenures" decreased. The "manse" explodes into small plots: mansions, courtils. The name "manse" eventually disappeared in areas of former settlement, while, resistant to fragmentation, it remained in the mountains in the form of "mas".

From the 9th century the allotment dominated in Auvergne as in southern France and the owner became a renter of the land. There has also been a progressive fragmentation and the village is a group of "independent owners of variable wealth".

It appears to be a free-ranging urban area, where dwellings were separated by open spaces, then the evolution was in the direction of a tightening and the creation of compact villages.

As the Christianization of the countryside intensified, small parishes, generally on the initiative of landowners, appeared alongside the large Merovingian parishes established in the vici, while monastic settlements multiplied.

These consecrated places, often fortified, places of asylum, provided with immunities by the sovereigns, attracted populations who found relative security among them.

This information, above, is important to explain that this family occupied the countryside between Saint Priest of the fields and Biollet in mansats (hamlets farms) (other families with the same patronymic occupied the areas of the communes of Les Ancizes-Comps, Saint Georges de Mons, Vitrac and Mansat.

Representation of the family tree

Antoine S. *1678-1748* & **Margueritte C.**

o Annet *1726-*
o Jean *1730-*
o Anne *1703 ?-1777* &27/4/1733 Gervais G
    Jean G 27/8/1734, Marie 4/7/1737, Jean 9/5/1742, Anne 8/11/1743

o **Marien 13/03/*1723-1780*** &1742 Magdeleine P 1720 (**mariage 1**)
    Gabriel 5/3/1746
    Anne 1754-1810 & Gervais C 1753
    Gervais 1751-178? &Anne G 1755
        Gabrielle 1784
        Gervais 1788 & Marie J-1850
            François 1817-1881 &1854 Anne P 1825
                Gabriel 1854 & 1887 Marie-Adèle P-1889
                    Jules Gabriel 1888
                    Marie-Louise 1889-1889
                Gabriel 1854 &1891 Marguerite Léontine P
                Gervais 1860
                Marie 1864
                Jean-Julien 1868
                Jean 1856 &1888 Marie S 1855
                    Marie-Gervaisine,
                    Félix-gervais,
                    Marie-Elisabeth,
                    Marie-Angèle,
                    Gervais 1893&Marie C
            Anne 1814 &1841 Philippe R 1813
            Gervais 1819-1886 & Marie G 1823-1847
            Gervais 1819-1886 & Anne L
                Marie 1855
                Jean 1859-1904 & 1887 Françoise T
                    Gervais
                    Gilbert 1853
                    François 1851&Françoise B 1858
                      Anne-Marie,
                      Etienne-François,
                      Jean 1887,
                    Jean 1907
o *Marien 1723-1780* & Marie B *1728-23/5/1763* (**mariage 2**)

o Jean *1761-*
o Amable *1762-1762*
o *Marien 1723-1780* &1765 **Anne L** *1728-* (**mariage 3**)
  o **Gervais** 16/4/*1766-1809* &1792? **Jeanne L** *10/1764-1801*
    o Henri *1796-*
    o Jean *1784-*
    o Gervais *1787-* &1810 Charlotte D *1786-*
      o Marien 23/9/*1815-* 1/5/1862& 17/1/1846 Marie M
                                     8/6/1822-27/3/1868
         o Gervais *1846-* & Anne C *1853-*
           o Jean *1871-*
           o André *1873-* &1891 Gilberte T
        o Pierre *1851-* & Marie S *1857-*
           o Marie *1878-*
           o Jean-Marie *1882-*
           o Eugène-André *1886-*
      o Gilberte *1818-* &1848 Jean L
      o Margueritte *1820-*
      o Anne *1823-*
      o André *1824-* & Marie L *1846-*
        o Francois *1848*
        o Marie *1857-* & Pierre S *1851-*
      o Amable *1827-*
  o Marien *1792-1869* & Marie L *1799-*
    o Gervais *1825*
    o Jean *1826-*
    o Antoinette *1828-* &1852 François C
    o Annet *1830-*
    o Gervais *1832-1883* &1869 Marie F *1847-*
      o Jacques *1864-* & Jeanne G *1862-*
        o Jean-Marie *1890-*
      o Francoise *1867-*
    o Antoinette *1832-*
    o Jean *1834-*
    o Henri *1836-* & Gabrielle P
      o Marie-Virginie *1862-* &1890 Pierre M
      o Amélie *1864-*
      o Jean *1867-* & Augustine F
        o Henri-Aimable *1893*
    o Jacques *1838-*
    o Marie *1840-*

o **Annet** *1793-* &1833 **Antoinette F** *1801-*
   o Marie *1836-* & André R *1836-*
   o Marie *1838*
   o Jacques *1842-*
   o Amable *1845-* & Marie S
      o Jean *1868-*
   o Gervais *1828-* & Marie B *1834-*
      o Marie *1859-* &1880 Antoine B *1859*
      o Jean *1862* & Amélie L 183
         Gervais 1893-1973&1935 Marie Francine C
         Marie-Gervaisine
         Marie-Elisabeth
         Marie-Angèle
      o Gervais *1864*
      o Gervais *1867-1868* & *1889 Marie B*
      Jean-Charles 1891-1977& 1919
               Marie- Jeanne P
   o Catherine *1830-*
o **Mathieu** *1833-1898* &1859 **Jeanne D** *1835-1899*
   o Pierre *1862-1868*
   o Claudine *1864-1864*
   o Hippolyte *1865-1868*
   o Jacques *1869-*
   o Jeanne *1870-1875*
   o Jeanne-Marie 1877-1877
   o **Jean-Marie** *1859-1905* &1883 **Benoite B**
                 1863- 1934
      o **Francoise** *1896-1898 (un fils Henri)*
      o **Joseph** *?1900-1905*
      o **Francois** *1901-*
      o **Jeanne-Francoise** *1884-1886*
      o **Antoine** *1886-1919*
      o **Jeanne** *1887-1910* &1905 **Jean B** *1880-*
      o **Jacques** *1891-1975* &1919 **Valentine D**
                 1898-1984
         o **Gaston** & **Suzanne X**
            2 enfants
         o **Louis-Antoine** *1894-1940* &1922
            avec **Jeanne R** *1896-1933*
         o **Lucien** & **Colette B** (3 enfants)

Explanations

► *Antoine S. 1678-1748 & Marguerite C.*

Antoine was born in the hamlet of La Roche (between Biollet and St Priest des champs). His brother Jean (1683-1733) nevertheless his younger brother stayed in this hamlet while he left a few hundred meters (or kilometers) further to the hamlet of La Brousse.
Antoine died at 70 and his brother Jean died at 50 (Jean's wife, Madeleine G., died at 60). Both were farmers. There would probably have been other children like Marien (1670) who would be the eldest son, married to Michelle D.

At that time, in this region, 80% of the people had died at 60 years of age and 50% of the people born reached 30 years of age.
Antoine therefore lived very old proof perhaps of a certain comfort.
In the Combraille region, 38 parishes, during the two periods 1738-1747 and 1771-1780, there were 3843 marriages, 17744 births, with 4.6 births per marriage. 18% of children died in the first year, 35% died before the age of 10, 50% died before the age of 30.
What were the causes of these deaths, often caused by disease? We can blame the lack of personal hygiene, unwashed clothes, dust and microbes nests; the crowding in which we lived at that time, the whole family occupied a single room where there was the greatest disorder; room ventilated only by a door, at most by a small narrow window; room in which we cooked, ate, slept, procreated, were born, were killed; a room on the ground of beaten clay on which the debris of the table was thrown, where dogs, cats and chickens circulated, a floor on which the filth of the farmyard was brought, with the hooves, which was on the same level as this unique room, sometimes doubled by another room, on the other side of the entrance, where hand tools, old

beds and many other scraps were stacked.

Antoine and Marguerite had 4 children:
 Anne (married in 1733 with Gervais G. They will have 4 children. Anne will live in a nearby hamlet which has the samename than the name of her husband. She will have lived more than 70 years.
 Annet born in 1726 died early
 John born in 1730 died early. Jean's godmother will be Antoine's brother's wife (i. e. Madeleine). This child therefore bears the first name of Antoine's brother.
 Marien (1/03/1723-1780), perhaps the second child (after his sister Anne), will be a labourer. He will live 57 years. It can be seen that births are quite spaced apart: the extremely cold winters of the early part of the century (the Little Ice Age) may be a plausible explanation.

▶   **Marien** is getting married three times. His role is important in this family because his children will settle in different sites of the Combrailles campaign.

1st wedding : **Marien** *1723-1780* & 1742 **Magdeleine P.** (1720-1759?, 39 years ?) 3 children
2nd wedding : **Marien** *1723-1780* & 1760 **Marie B.** *1728-1763* 2 children
3rd wedding : **Marien** *1723-1780* & 1765 **Anne** L. (1726) 1 child

 Marien married at the age of 19, which is very early for the time when men were married around 25, less than 4 years later a son Gabriel (5/3/1746) was born who died, then 5 years later a second son Gervais 1751-178? (he was 29 years old when his father died) and 3 years later a daughter Anne 1754-1810 (died at 56, she was 5 years old when her mother died)- Anne married Gervais C. and had a son Gervais, a soldier in the 1st Scout Regiment, Napoleon's campaign 1813, 1814.

 Births are still very distant, but there have been successive periods of very great famines.

6 years after Anne's birth, Marien remarried at 37, he would have two children Jean 1761- and Amable 1762-1762 both died at birth. Their mother Mary died 1 year later at 35 years of age)
(winter was very cold)
Less than two years after the death of his second wife, he remarried at 43 years of age in 1765 with Anne L. : one year later, they had a son Gervais (16/4/1766-14/12/1809). Gervais will live 43 years. He was 14 years old when his father died. The civil status records indicate that he is an owner farmer.

Anne (daughter from the 1st marriage married quite late, she may have been prevented from doing so to raise the children and keep the house because Gervais (3rd marriage) was 14 years old when her father died and 21 at her sister Anne's wedding (but this is only a guess)

Gervais was a first name given to each generation on all branches of the tree.

What has happened during this century that could explain these events?

1723	naissance Marien	1722-1723, 1725-1726 Eté caniculaire
1742	**1er mariage**	1742 été caniculaire
1746	naissance de Gabriel décédé	Famine suite aux étés chauds
1751	naissance de Gervais (mort à 33 ans)	1750-1752 grandes famines
1754	naissance de Anne (morte à 56 ans)	
1769 ?	décès de sa femme ?	1769-1770 grandes famines
1760	**2ème mariage**	été caniculaire
1761	Jean décédé	été caniculaire
1762	Amable décédé	hiver froid, neige, gelées, automne mouillé, été chaud
1764 ?	décès de sa femme ?	année très froide mais été chaud
1765	**3ème mariage**	hiver très froid, été humide
1766	naissance de Gervais (mort à 33 ans)	hiver très froid
1780	mort de Marien	printemps chaud suivi d'un été très chaud
1809	mort de Gervais (3ème mariage)	cet hiver a été exceptionnellement doux
1810	mort de Anne (1er mariage)	hiver sec et froid

▶ Study of Gervais, son from Marien's first marriage

This branch will live in a hamlet near the hamlets of La Brousse and La Roche called Puy-Pelat and in the village of Laussedat.

> (1) **Gervais** 14/5/1751-178? & Anne G 1755- ?
> He was a landowner and farmer
> They will have 2 children:
> **Gabrielle** 1784   deceased at birth
> (2) **Gervais** 1788-1819 ? (31 years?) & Marie J. 1788-2/5/1850
> (died at 62 years of age)

(2) **Gervais** 1788-1819 ? He died in the city of Blois, he was probably a mason,

They will have had 4 children: Anne, François, Gervais (3) born in the year of his father's death, raised by their mother and grandparents.

The boys will be masons: "Why did they change from owner farmer to mason? »

> **Anne** 3/5/1814 & 13/2/1841 Philippe R. 29/7/1813
> Anne is the eldest, she got married at 27, quite late
> **Robert** ?
> **François** 1817-1881 &1854 Anne P 1825

François will be a mason, he will marry at 37 years old in 1854, quite late, he will live 64 years old. They will have 5 children:

> Gabriel 1854 married in 1887 with Marie-Adèle P-1889
> At first farmer then mason, 1.63m
> He will be a mason and will migrate to Fleurie in Beaujolais
> He will marry twice at 33. and at 37.
> His two children died at birth, his wife probably died as a result of the birth on 25/5/1889. She is pregnant immediately after the birth and death of Jules Gabriel
> > Jules Gabriel 18/6/1888
> > Marie-Louise 2/4/1889-7/10/1889
> Gabriel's marriage in 1891 to Marguerite Léontine P, ironer.

> Gervais 1860 died at birth
> Mary 1864 died at birth
> Jean-Julien 1868 mason - 1,67m

Jean 23/7/1856 &17/1/1/1888 Marie S 19/11/1855
Jean was a mason, he married his cousin, daughter of
Gervais (François' brother) below (1819-1886) at the
age of 32. They will have 6 children:
  Marie-Gervaisine 6/9/1886 died early
  Félix-Gervais 10/11/1889, farmer, 1m71,
  deceased 3/10/1929 at Verghéas
  Mary Elizabeth, 8/11/1888 died early
  Mary Angela, 10/8/1891 early death
  Francisque Félix 26/12/1897, farmer, 1m60
  Gervais 18/8/1893-1973 & 30/11/1935 with
Marie C. who died on 11/10/1973 at Biollet.
He got married at 42
> Félix-Gervais and Francisque-Félix have restarted farming

(3) Gervais 24/14/1819-28/10/1886 & Marie G 1823-1847
  First marriage
  He will live 67 years
  Marie G died at 24, they won't have children
(3) Gervais 1819-1886 & 11/2/1851 Anne L
  He is 32 years old at his second marriage; they will have
  4 children:
Mary 19/11/1855 will marry Jean son of François, she is 33 years old at the time of
her marriage
John 6/1/1/1859-7/7/1904 & 4/7/1887 Françoise T.
He married at the age of 28, a bricklayer, and died at the age of 45 in Fleurie in
Beaujolais. He got married at 28.
  They would have a son Gervais who died in 1886
Gilbert 7/6/1853 died at birth
François 14/11/1851 & Françoise B. 1858
  He is a farmer
  Anne-Marie 1/12/1884
  Etienne-François 1891, farmer, 1m66
  John 1887, farmer, 1m59
  Jean 1907, farmer (he did his service military in Lyon Bron)
> Etienne-François and Jean have also taken up farming again

Remark: the cousins saw each other frequently and visibly influenced
each other in terms of professions and places of travels (Fleurie)

What happened from a meteorological point of view during these periods :

1784	naissance et décès de Gabrielle	hiver très rigoureux, été froid et humide
1788	naissance de Gervais	hiver doux, énorme grêle en Puy de Dôme
1814	naissance de Anne	hiver rude
1817	naissance de François	été caniculaire
1819	naissance de Gervais	périodes de froids intenses
1846	1er mariage de Gervais avec Marie G	été caniculaire
1847	mort de Marie G	hiver très rigoureux
1841	mariage de Anne et Philippe R	très froid et pluvieux en hiver et en été
1851	2ème mariage de Gervais avec Anne L	très froid et pluvieux en hiver et en été
1851	naissance de François	très froid et pluvieux en hiver et en été
1853	naissance et mort de Gilbert	froid en hiver, frais en été
1854	mariage de François et Anne P	hiver rigoureux, printemps humide, été frais
1854	naissance de Gabriel	hiver rigoureux, printemps humide, été frais
1856	naissance de Jean	froid et pluvieux
1859	naissance de Jean	été très chaud
1860	mort à la naissance de Gervais	très froid été comme hiver
1864	mort à la naissance de Marie	vague de froid l'hiver, très chaud l'été
1868	mort à la naissance de Jean-Julien	vague de froid l'hiver, très chaud l'été
1884	naissance de Anne Marie	hiver doux, été chaud mais tardif
1886	mort tôt de Marie Gervaisine	froid, pluvieux, été tardif
1887	naissance de Jean	glacial l'hiver, chaud l'été
1887	1 er mariage de Gabriel avec Marie Adèle	glacial l'hiver, chaud l'été
1887	mariage de Jean avec Françoise T	glacial l'hiver, chaud l'été
1888	mariage de Jean et de Marie S	très froid été comme hiver
1889	mort de Marie Adèle et de ses 2 enfants en 1888 et 1889	très froid été comme hiver
1889	naissance de Félix Gervais	très froid été comme hiver
1891	2ème mariage de Gabriel avec Marguerite Léontine	vague de froid, été pourri
1891	mort tôt de Marie Angèle	vague de froid, été pourri
1891	naissance de Etienne François	vague de froid, été pourri
1893	naissance de Gervais	hiver froid mais été très chaud
1897	naissance de Francisque Félix	hiver doux, été plutôt chaud
1904	mort de Jean	pluvieux, canicule en été
1907	naissance de Jean	vague de froid et été frais
1935	mariage de Gervais avec Marie C.	vague de froid au printemps, été froid

The 19th century was subject to rather harsh weather conditions with harsh winters and cool, humid summers, while in the 18th century there were many heat waves.
High mortality is observed during cold periods.

In this branch of the tree of this family, the men were masons. They may have lost their property or been unable to cultivate their land. Around 1900, several men returned to farming.
In the middle of the 19th century, there were permanent departures to Fleurie in Beaujolais (Gabriel and Jean, they were masons). All these cousins obviously saw each other regularly and talked, perhaps they went to work together and in the same places.

Men married quite late, it is due to both their profession and the fact that they did military service of 2 to 5 years or more)
The other remarkable feature is that they died quite early.

The hardship of travelling or working in a profession can be one of the causes, as well as poor nutrition and very difficult weather conditions. Another explanation is that migrants reported unknown germs on bodies that could not heal, medicine at the time had only ineffective remedies at its disposal.
Men died early and lived shorter lives than in the 18th century. The children were therefore orphaned at a very early age, raised by the mother and the first family circle. However, it should be remembered that since school is not compulsory, children worked very young.
We observe several remarriages, and one marriage between cousins.
Women died in childbirth for the reasons we will explain:

The midwives, called "accoucheuses" in the land of Combraille, were under the supervision and close dependence of the clergy. From the same period as surgeons (first quarter of the 18th century, aspiring midwives had to produce certificates of good conduct issued by the priest and the judge of the localities where they wanted to practise. They were examined on the principles of their art and paid 15 to 50 pounds of reception fees. These are only sworn midwives. In fact, it seems that none of them attended the school founded in Clermont for them. The clergy especially ensures that midwives know how to administer baptism to a child in danger of death in an emergency. In this case it must do so in the presence of a witness. The bishop asked about their abilities, especially towards the end of the 18th century. In reality, these women were poorly educated in their art and practiced only routinely, although an attempt had been made by the intendants of Auvergne to raise the level, but it does not seem to have reached the midwives of the Combraille region.
During the 1729 pilgrimage, Bishop Massillon pointed out in

most parishes that there were no sufficiently educated midwives and even no midwives at all. In Saint Priest des Champs, for example, in 1784, there was only one educated midwife. There were very few registered midwives for nearly 1500 births per year in this region. These women therefore had a lot of work given the number of children per woman (4.6). He died many children, 18.57% in the first months due to the lack of care of the midwife who did not know what to do in this or that difficult case and not helped by mothers who were ignorant and who only had in childcare the lights of the grandmother who had survived or the old neighbour who predicted appropriate and unknown cures. From two to ten years old, 12% of children were still suffering from childhood epidemic diseases, most often benign today. A total of 42.5% of children did not reach adult age. Young mothers, always for lack of appropriate hygienic care, were at risk of death during childbirth and especially in the days following delivery: puerperal fever[29] was common due to the absence of known disinfectants and the inability of midwives. But one of the main causes is the lack of hygiene in general and physical hygiene in particular.

The women remained alone for a very long time and managed the affairs and were in charge of the children's education.

---

29 La *fièvre puerpérale* est un état pathologique qui résulte, généralement, d'une infection des voies génitales de la femme
Puerperal fever is a condition that usually results from an infection of the female genital tract.

The Combrailles region had a lot of people who went to work outside the region, it was the price to pay to survive. Agriculture was no longer enough to live on.

The climatic conditions between very harsh winters and heat waves resulted in famine.

The Cantal and Puy de Dôme regions supplied loggers and pitsawyers.

The southern part of the Creuse region is the construction workers.

Cantal, a poor region, provided a large quantity of workers for the hardest and most poorly paid urban works.

All these migrants left at the rhythm of the seasons, usually in winter because there was nothing to do in that season, but others in summer depending on the profession.

The seasonal exodus was part of an annual rhythm that intensified with the progress of the means of communication, the creation of roads, railway lines and the modernization of the modes of transport.

This progress increased the number of departures.

But these migrants travelled on foot, poorly equipped, they still travelled 40 to 50 kilometres a day, following traditional routes, travelling in groups, often from the same village or region.

These migrations contributed very little to cultural change, and village solidarity is strongly present. Integration at the beginning of the 19th century was weak, the masons for example remained among themselves, spoke their own language, lived in the same house.

Even if their eyes remained fixed on their native land, migrants inadvertently became agents of modernization contributing to the economic and cultural enrichment of their villages.

This impermeability was breaking down more and more quickly. Emigration thus helped to ease the labour market and spread new ideas.

The worker returning home would teach his relatives that there was something different elsewhere.

Migration, in both seasonal and non-seasonal forms, had always included an element of adventure. Leaving home was an act of anxiety, but also an event and a liberation, a way to escape the conditions of rural life.

The young mason could leave at the age of 14. Not only was he no longer a mouth to feed, he was going to bring in extra income.

Migration also advanced alphabetization because migrants felt that writing, reading and numeracy were useful for their work, and allowed them to keep in touch with their families through mail.

This migration also facilitated the spread of new ideas, but "what is fundamental is not the arrival of new ideas, but the emergence of conditions such that these ideas can be well received "[30].

---

30 Maurice Agulhon, historien (né le 20/12/196 à Uzès (Gard), mort le 28/5/201) à Brignoles dans le Var)

Some comments on the social condition of children in the 19th century

Victor Hugo, a writer, protested against child labour and called for education for all. Through his literary work, he was able to highlight the different aspects of childhood in the 19th century, through Gavroche, Eponine, Azelma, Cosette. His influence in raising awareness of this social phenomenon was great.

In the 19th century, if the bourgeois family cared for their children and cared about the professional future of their children, the working and peasant families had survival as their main concern. These families live in a single room with poor furniture; the family, large, is a victim of the industrial revolution. The exploitation of children in the workplace is a dramatic reality, but thanks to school and social laws in favour of minors, it is gradually declining until it becomes, at the end of the 19th century, a marginal reality. The Republican school is a factor in social promotion, but this movement will be very slow and will remain very unequal.

In the city, the poor child's education is mainly in the street or at work and gradually at school.

The little beggar is present throughout the century. He is not an occasional beggar, but a child forced to ask for charity from passers-by in both summer and winter. Chased away by the police, he moves from one district to another. The ultimate punishment is to force him to go to school. As Victor Hugo describes it, the wandering child wanders in the cities. There are also children who are victims of real trafficking and are sold by families too poor to feed them and sent to distant regions. They are often forced to perform degrading or dangerous tasks. The "children of the Empire" are taken from their native land to serve in colonized countries. Others end up in prison for delinquency: petty thieves, prostituted girls, accomplices of adult criminals.

Children are employed at a very young age in roads, tobacco factories and cotton mills. The working day is 14 to 16 hours at a salary four times lower than the wage of an adult. Maltreated, poorly clothed and poorly fed, they have to walk, from three in the morning, the long distance between their house and their workshop and make the opposite way in the evening, after a tiring day's work. In the mines, they are used (sometimes as young as four years old) to crawl through narrow galleries, tied like animals to the cart pushed by another child. Their task is to open and close the doors of the galleries, forcing them to remain alone underground for ten to twelve hours.

Antoine Sylvère's autobiographical book, "Toinou" teaches us about the living conditions of an Auvergne child in the 19th century. This book sheds light on the living conditions of peasants, on the great desolation of children without joy, beaten, exploited, recruited at the factory.

Toinou reports on what his young years were like in an environment of social misery. Violence against him, humiliations, punishments are part of his daily life. Abused by his parents, abused at school, he has nothing to expect from life, he knows neither joy nor hope. The world is divided into two clans, one of the rich and the other of the poor. This realistic painting, worthy of Zola's writings, is a testimony of great quality, lived from the inside. Toinou refused his condition and by force of tenacity succeeded in undertaking studies. If this social novel is black and realistic, it also brings hope.

Extract: "This education fortunately prepared us for the beast of burden that our parents led. She accustomed us to bear without complaints, if not without pain, the injustices that would be our lot; to bear them, especially, without revolt, because that is indeed the most detestable way to complain.

The Brothers' school thus provided the local bourgeoisie with a large supply of adolescents prepared for their future role as workers and sharecroppers without demands, silent, submissive, fearful. The blows, administered at any time and out of place, imposed on the child a kind of dark fatalism which, combined with a whole system of degrading humiliations, gradually made him a weak and cowardly being. »

► Study of the family tree of Marien's third marriage

o Marien 1723-1780 (57 years old) & 1765 (43 years old) Anne L 1728- (marriage 3)
Only one child was born, Marien was 43 years old,
The age of death of Anne L. is unknown.
They live in the village of La Brousse, he was a farmer.

o Gervais (1) 16/4/1766-1809 &? Jeanne L. 10/1764-1801

It is indicated that he is the owner. He was 14 years old when his father died in 1780
He died at 43 (8 years after his wife). He will have 5 children with Jeanne L.
They got married early and Jeanne was two years older.

The first son Jean was born in 1784, Gervais (1) was 18 years old, and Jeanne 20 years old
Then Gervais (2) will come in 1787, Gervais (1) will be 21 years old
then will come Marien in 1792, Gervais (1) will be 26 years old
then Annet will come in 1793, Gervais (1) will be 27 years old
then Henri will come in 1796, Gervais (1) will be 30 years old, Anne 32 years old
Jeanne died 5 years later at 37 years of age
Gervais died 8 years after his wife

They will therefore have 5 children, 5 sons:
> o Henry 1796 - probably died at birth
> o John 1784 - probably died at birth

The first and last son died at birth
> o Gervais (2) 6/3/1787- &1810 Charlotte D. 1786-

Gervais (2) is 23 years old at the time of his marriage, he is owner - farmer and
Charlotte at 24 years old, They will have 6 children including 3 living:
> o Marian 1815- 1862 & 1846 with Marie M. 1822-1868

Marien is a mason, he gets married at 31 years old in winter on January 17, Mary is
24 years old.
He will die at 47, Mary will die at 46. They will have 2 children:
> o Gervais (3) 23/9/1846-1883 & married in 1870 with
> Anne C. 1853- 1882

Gervais (3) will be a mason, 1m63, he is 16 years old at the death of his father
Gervais (3) will die at 37, 1 year after his wife, Anne his wife will die at 29
They are respectively 24 and 17 years old at their marriage.
They will have 2 children (boys)
> o Jean 25/12/1871- married on 12/1/1896 with

Françoise N., he is 25 years old at his marriage

It is indicated that he is a mason, chief farmer, 1.69m.
He was 12 years old when his father died and 11 years old when his mother died.

o André 1873-1908 married in 1891 with
Gilberte T. in the town of Oullins near Lyon.
He's a mason, he's 19 years old at his wedding, he died of tuberculosis at 28
o Pierre 1851- married in 1878 with Marie S. 1857-
died before 1902
Youngest brother of Gervais (3), mason, 1,63m
He was 11 years old when his father died and 17 years old when his mother died.
At the age of 27, he married his cousin (she was 21), daughter of André, brother of his
father Marien.)   They will have 3 children:
o Mary 1878-
o Jean-Marie 1882- mason, 1,65m
veteran 14-18
o Eugène-André 1886 mason-1,68m
veteran 14-18

o Gilberte 1818- &1848 Jean L.
Gilberte daughter of Gervais (2) and Charlotte D. She married at 30 years old
o Margueritte 1820-
o Anne 1823-
o André 1824- & married 28/8/1842 Marie L 1846-
He married at 18, Mary at 24; they have 2 children (the differences are significant)
o Francois 1848
o Marie 1857, died before 1902 & 1878 Pierre S
1851- (married with his cousin Pierre)
o Amable 1827-died probably in 1868 (41 years old)

o Marien son of Gervais (1) 1792-1868 & married in 1826 with
Marie L 1799-
Hamlet of Cordaleix, he died at 77, married at 34, he was a farmer
o Gervais 1825
o Jean 1826-
o Antoinette (married at 24)1828- &1852 François C
o Annet 1830-
o Gervais 1832-1883 (51 years old) & 1869 Marie F 1847-
He is a farmer
he married at 37, 9 months after the death of his father Marien. He was capable of
signing. Marie was 22 years old. A marriage contract has been established.

They lived in the hamlet of Comdoubex near the village of Biollet: a boy and a girl

> *o Jacques 1864- married at 24 in 1888 with*
> *Jeanne G 1862- He is a farmer*
> *military service in the infantry*
> > *o Jean-Marie 1890- (1.81m, farmer)*
> > *artillery regiment - war wound*
> > *veteran 14-18*
> > *o Francois 1867-1m76, farrier*
> > *military service in artillery*

> o Antoinette 1832-
> o John 1834-
> o Henri 1836- & Gabrielle P
> > *o Marie-Virginie 1862- (married at 27 years old)*

in 1890 with Pierre M. 25 years old
> > *o Amélie 1864-1873 died at the age of 9*
> > *o John 1867- & Augustine F 1867*
> > > *o Henri-Aimable 1893,*
> > > *farmer and bricklayer, single,*
> > > *Corporal 1914, deadly war wound,*
> > > *buried in Germany*

> o James 1838-
> o Mary 1840-

o Annet 1793- &1833 Antoinette F. 1801-
Farmer in La Brousse, died at 69 years old, married at 32 years old, Antoinette was 24 years old at the time of the marriage.
They had 8 children:
> o 4- Mary 1836 who died early
> o 5- Marie 1838- marriage at 27 years old with André R

1836-
> o 2- Catherine 1830-
> o 6- Mary 1840 who died early
> o 7- Jacques 1842- mason
> o 8-Amable 1845 mason - married with Marie S
> > o John 1868-
> o 1- Gervais 1828- 1867 mason & Marie B 1834-

He died at the age of 39. His wife was 33 years old. They had 4 children:
> > o 1- Marie 1859- married at 24 in 1880 with
> > > Antoine B 1859
> > o 2- Jean 1862 mason & Amélie L

They had 4 children
- 4-Gervais 1893-1973 married in 1935 with
Marie Francine C.
He got married at 42
War 14-18, Corporal, 16 RI, war cross with bronze star, multiple wounds, he was 21
years old at the beginning of the war
-1- Marie-Gervaisine 1886
-2- Marie-Elisabeth 1888
-3- Marie-Angèle 1891

o Gervais 1864 mason, died in 1886 in
Chaumont Hospital (at 24 years old)
Her birth was declared by the midwife in September
o Gervais 1867- married at 21 in 1889 with
Marie B, in Fleurie (Rhône), 1 child:
°Jean-Charles 1891-1977 (died at 86)
married at 28 in 1919 with Marie-Jeanne P in Fleurie (Rhône)

Discussion: the first name Gervais is broadcast very regularly. They are masons by profession and die quite early; a branch of the tree has remained in agriculture. In this profession they lived longer, which could mean that they were financially better off. The war caused several branches to stop. Their level of education is 3 (reading and writing)

o 3- Mathieu 1833-1898 married in 1859 with Jeanne D. 1835-
1899
Son of Annet and Antoinette F., he left Biollet between 1851 and 1856 (he was about
20 years old) for Beaujeu. He will live to be 65 (his wife Jeanne will also die at 65)
and he got married at 26.
Mason, he couldn't sign at his marriage.
They will have 7 children:
He will be 29 years old when his father dies.
Children in rank 2, 3, 4, 4, 6, 7 will die very early
There will only be two boys left: Jean-Marie and Jacques (10 years younger than
Jean-Marie)

O 2- Pierre 1862-1868 (died at age 6)
o 3- Claudine 1864-1864 (death at birth)
o 4- Hippolyte 1865-1868 (décès à 3 ans)

o 5- *Jacques 1869- mason, 1m74, 5th regiment of*
cuirassiers. He will be 29 years old when his father dies (like his father when his
father dies); his level of education is 2.
o 6- *Jeanne 1870-1875 died at 5 years old*
o 7- *Jeanne-Marie 1877-1877 deaths: birth*
o 1- *Jean-Marie 1859-1905 &1883 Benoite B*
1863- 1934 - He died at 46, he married at 24. Benoite died at 71
She was 42 years old when her husband died. She was a cleaning lady.
They had 8 children:
o 6- *Francoise 1896-1898*
(died at 2 years old)
o 7- *Joseph ?1900-1905 died 5 years ago,*
the year his father died
o 8- *Francois 1901-*
o 1- *Jeanne-Francoise 1884-1886*
(died at 4 years old)
o 2 - *Antoine 1886-1919, mason, 1m73*
War 14-18, prisoner of war in St Hilaire the Great,
died in Lyon in 1919 at the age of 33, a few days after his
death., *back, he was a breadwinner,*
he was 19 years old when his father died
o 3- Jeanne 1887-1910 married in 1905
with Jean B 1880-
Married at 18, died at 23 of illness at the Beaujeu hospital
Marriage the same year as his father's death - a son Henri in 1907 abandoned
At the end of the same year his brother Joseph died
o Jacques 1891-1975 &1919 Valentine D
1898-1984, died at 84 years old, married at 28 years old, volunteered at 18 years old in
the Cuirassiers in Lyon, veteran, prisoner of war in Germany, 1m71
He will be a tinsmith in St Didier sur Beaujeu
He was 14 years old when his father died: they will have 1 son
o Gaston 1920-1977 (died at 57)
married with Suzanne X, they will
have 2 children
o Louis-Antoine 1894-1940, married at 28
in 1922 with Jeanne R 1896-1933; Jeanne died at 37 in Villefranche sur Saône of a
peritonitis; only 10 years of marriage,volunteered at 18 years old in the Cuirassiers in
Lyon, veteran, military, spahis in Morocco and Algeria, war 14-18, battle of Verdun,
army of the East
 They will have one son: Lucien 1924 married in 1949 with Colette B (they will have
3 children)

Some explanations:
Louis-Antoine, 1m75 tall, died at 46, married at 28. His son Lucien was 16 years old when his father died and 9 years old when his mother died. Louis-Antoine joined the 10th regiment of cuirassiers in Lyon at the age of 18, then the 1st regiment of Moroccan spahis, then the 5th regiment of Algerian spahis, the Verdun campaign, then the army of the East in Macedonia, the return will take place in 1919; he will go to the gendarmerie school. He will be in the Gendarmerie on horseback at the 7th Legion.
He was reactivated in 1938 and died of tuberculosis in 1940. He was a blacksmith, a housing marshal.
Military Medal - Colonial medal with Moroccan clasp

In 1939, Louis-Antoine enrolled his son in the Naval Academy of Lorient, Lucien was 16 years old. At the age of 18 in 1940, he was sent to the Algiers Navy unit in Senegal, Morocco, Mauritania and Madagascar. He left the French Navy in 1949 at the age of 25 (Louis-Antoine left the army to join the Gendarmerie in 1921 at the age of 27). Lucien left the Navy permanently (military periods) in 1965 at the age of 41 (Louis-Antoine was released from his duties in the Gendarmerie in 1939 at the age of 45).

Additional information:

Mathieu (and his descendants) when he arrived at Beaujeu lived in the "Pont Paradis" district near a tannery, which may explain the high mortality rates. At the death of her husband Jean-Marie, Benoite lived on Place de l'Eglise in Beaujeu, his resources were more than modest, his work as a household help and washerwoman was not enough to support the family properly. The eldest son, a family breadwinner, probably suffered from this situation. The voluntary commitment of the three sons is a way out of this social situation.

Discussions

What do we discover in this family tree?

The origins of the family are peasant, whose homeland is the region of "Combrailles auvergnates" (Biollet, Saint Priest des champs).
They were farmers, labourers and owners for the most part until the 18th century. Life expectancy was 40 or 70 years, and the mortality rate was consistent with the rate at that time[31].

The tree is characterized by the 3 remarriages of Marien 1723-1780.
It is interesting to note the similarity of the situations of each of the branches of the tree with remarriages due to death, two marriages between cousins, migrations at the same time and to the same places.
At the beginning of the 19th century, we observe changes: men become masons[32] and thus we record departures from the region, at the beginning of short periods, then definitive especially in the middle of the century following a general trend.
The 18th and 19th centuries saw severe economic difficulties, very hot summers, very harsh winters and deadly famines. Living conditions were very difficult.

What characterizes this family is that almost all men are masons. At the end of the 19th century, blacksmiths and soldiers were observed.
Travel was frequent, distant and of varying lengths. So they married late and died early.
It must be taken into account that they have often served in the military for a long time.

---

31 50% des enfants ne dépassaient pas l'age de 10 ans.
32 En Combrailles beaucoup furent maçons et migrèrent vers la région de Lyon et du Beaujolais, alors qu'en Creuse du sud, beaucoup furent aussi maçons mais migrèrent vers Paris

Their wives therefore remained widows for a long time unless they died in childbirth. Due to their husbands' absences, women were most often left alone to care for children and household or farm matters.

While infant mortality was very high, children were orphaned at a very early age, raising the question of child rearing.

In terms of repetition of life scenarios, in addition to the unique profession (mason), it can practically be said that they were orphans from father to son.

These repetitions of first names, situations, professions, traumas, are revelations of the elements that will build the unconscious family; all these waves will spread from generation to generation.

They have no choice but to work as masons, to leave, to marry late, to die early.

Children are conceived upon the father's return, after the death of a child, the surrogate child is born with the same first name, as in all families. Pregnancies and probably childbirths occur without the presence of the father; the child's acceptance into life is without the tenderness of a home. The happy event of a birth is often overshadowed by an event, the death of a loved one, famine. Because one or both parents died early, the eldest daughter or son becomes the head of the family and devotes himself to the education of the children, and gets married late.

From a theoretical point of view, age differences are also interesting information that can be divided into three groups:

An age gap between 0 and 3 years allows for good sibling relationships, friendship and complicity.

In the case of an age difference of three to seven years, a natural virtual balance of power is applied.

If the gap is more than seven years, it is a virtual parent relationship between the oldest and youngest.

Relationships had to be made according to this distinction, considering that even if the gap was small, given the high infant mortality, the gap could have been large; one can move from case 1 to case 3 knowing that the deceased child will keep his place. This last point is important because in this numerological or chronological symbolism, the place gives a simplified character[33]:

The Elder: Entrepreneur and Leader Role
The cadet: role of advisor, conciliator
The third: communication role, facilitator
The fourth: organizer is the place of the holder of family fears
The fifth: very mobile and adaptable, versatile
The sixth: it is the tender, the sensual
The seventh: he is in love with knowledge
The eighth: brave, powerful
The ninth: it is the wise, humanism
The tenth one symbolically takes up the criteria of the first one

As an example 1, Jean-Marie 1859-1905 had 8 children:
The first Jeanne-Françoise died at the age of 2
The second Antoine, who died at the age of 33, was in charge of the family (he therefore exercised the role of head of the family and conciliator)
The third Jeanne died at the age of 23, she would have had a communication role in this symbolic role

---

33 Danielle Nicouleau "Etre sans ses ancêtre", 2004, Editions Presse du Midi

The fourth was Jacques who died at 84 years of age (family fears)
Le cinquième est Louis-Antoine (militaire) (rôle : très mobile, adaptable, polyvalent : c'est vrai, militaire, gendarme, maréchal-ferrant, il a beaucoup voyagé)
Le sixième est Françoise décédée à 2 ans(rôle :c'est la tendre)
Le septième, Joseph mort à 5 ans (rôle : épris de connaissance)
Le huitième, François mais pas d'information sur lui

Example 2 :

If we go back a generation (to Jean-Marie's father's level above, i. e. Mathieu 1838-1898, he had 6 children:
The first is Jean-Marie, who died at the age of 45, (role of the head, of the entrepreneur)-this is Jean-Marie from the previous case-
The second Pierre, died at the age of 6, (role of head of family and conciliator)
The third Claudine died at the age of 2, she would have had a communication role in this symbolic role
The fourth was Hippolyte who died at the age of 3 (family fears)
The fifth is Jacques (he was a soldier) (role: very mobile, adaptable, versatile): this is the position of Louis-Antoine, also a military in the previous example!
The sixth one died at 1 year old Jeanne (role: it is the tender one)

Example 3 :

Let's go back another generation, to Annet's 1793-1862 level
He had 8 children:
The first Gervais died at 39 years old (role of the chief)
The second Catherine, died early (role: head of family and conciliator)
The third Mathieu died at 54 years of age, (communication role,[he is the one who migrated definitively in example 2])
The fourth is Mary who died early (role: holder of family fears)

The fifth is Mary, married, (role: very mobile, adaptable, versatile)

The sixth is Mary who died early (role: it is the tender one)
The seventh, Jacques, mason (role: knowledge-loving)
The eighth, Amable, mason, married (role: humanism)

According to this symbolic statement, the death of the first children can have a significant psychological impact on the family's balance, as can Mathieu's departure from the region of birth.

Lucien (1924), son of Louis-Antoine, is an only child, his mother having died when he was 9 years old. His father being a gendarme, his parents moved as he was assigned. Lucien's situation is not privileged because he did not have the means to share with a brother or sister, he is the sole role holder.

The difficulties of his situation (orphan) give him an adult role very early on, with adult responsibilities and an obligation to be autonomous.

Anyone who has suffered from a lack of child care and therefore siblings will try to marry a partner from a large sibling to compensate.

This is the case here, Lucien will marry Colette, the eldest of 12 children. This alliance offered him a new opportunity, a favourable ground or rather a soil favourable to the more harmonious redeployment of his tree. This marriage made it possible to regenerate and oxygenate his tree in such a way that the new sprouts are made in favourable contexts leading to positive goals.

His son was born on the same day and month as Mathieu, his great-grandfather. His first name will take up a usual first name from Lucien's mother's tree, perhaps proof that education was provided by this family circle. But in this family too, the men, although belonging to a line of artisans, died early. The word orphan has a powerful meaning here.

If Lucien is the only son, Gaston his cousin, son of Jacques, who is Louis-Antoine's brother, is also the only son. Professional and family life "injured", he died at 57 years of age leaving two children, two years after his father's death and at the same age as his distant ancestor Marien 1723-1780 (the one who had 3 marriages).

The tree was, at this level, sick, he did not meet the structuring tree allowing him to generate a healing at the psychological level.

The first name Gervais was used for a long time; it was lost when the "tree" deviated to another region. This first name may reveal an ancestor whom we seek to venerate or thank, perhaps it is the one who settled in the region before the 18th century, or a Gervais who was noticed during the French revolution (at the same time one was the owner and a cousin died in Blois). This repetition is not a fashionable phenomenon but really an unconscious family obligation. The first names from the family tree such as Annet, Marien, Antoine, Gervais, seem to have been imposed by the father at least for the first children. For the following children in the chronology, we find first names more frequently given in the mothers' family trees. This trend is accentuated with time, geographical distance and the disappearance of the father before birth.

Children were rarely alone, they occupied a place in a family, even in the absence of the father or mother.

Chronology gives him a rank and gives him responsibilities that influence his life very early on. Nowadays, the family unit is restricted to parents and siblings. In earlier times and given the conditions mentioned, the family circle was larger and extended to grandparents, cousins, or even there was another circle including the neighbours living in the hamlet or village.

In the absence of both father and mother, the education of the children was carried out by the community. This group, which constitutes this community, plays an essential role; this group is a privileged and familiar place where children can experience their relationships with others, in which they build a living space closely linked to the relationships they establish with an environment that soothes them despite the importance and weight of the difficulties they face.

In these family trees above, there are no ghosts: no theft, murder, delinquency... Thus a balanced system of interdependence and solidarity is established. The behaviour of each individual is determined by the way the group represents the external environment and the meaning that this environment has for the group.

They were mostly masons, some migrated together to the same place. The distant cousins in the family tree stayed very close and talked to each other. This family group therefore had its own unique dynamic. Members of the tree from Marien's first marriage migrated to Fleurie in Beaujolais, members of Marien's third marriage migrated to Beaujeu. Except Fleurie and Beaujeu are only a few kilometers away. Did they continue to see each other or were the communication channels and networks broken?

Behaviourist models in social psychology assume that a person's social behaviour is determined by external influences considered as determining factors. In our examples, the family group extended to the first and second circle is stable and repetitive. However, these men travel, are provided with external information and new images, but when they join the group they are taken up by ancestral and natural ties.

In reality, the behaviour of these people depends more on mental processes than on external influences, i.e. on how they integrate the elements of information from the environment into a psychic element by treating them according to complex operating modes that allow them to understand social reality and give them meaning. These people were concerned about protecting themselves from the difficulties of the outside world, especially since they had a lot to do with their own difficulties.

For generations, the family group has defined its own processes for processing and integrating information, and has implemented its own cognitive constructions of reality.

The extended family group is the guarantor of the family history, it collects the information and gives it back with biases but the reading grid is only available to the members of the group.

At the beginning of the 19th century, these men and women could neither read nor write, so the transmission of the coding of comprehension was important, coding signs, certainties, fuzzy, unsaid, sighs, cries.

The testimonies validate the statements and consolidate the group. At some point there's a change. What was the catalyst, intervention or set of actions that triggered an individual change? Was it by decision of the group, under pressure from economic situations, for example, that one of the members decided to migrate and then settle down?

The tree was socially "modest", nothing that could restore the "coat of arms" or satisfy a certain family myth. The striking fact of this tree in the broadest sense would be the word absence: men were absent for a long time and perhaps this was the cause of their early death. Even now the members of the tree still have a taste for travel, for business trips.

How can this mortality be explained?

Probably because it does not take into account the microbes brought back with the money by temporary migrants.

Lack of hygiene and poor nutrition were an open door to disease. Thus infectious germs killed families. But it is now difficult to know these diseases outside the normal endemics of certain regions, chronic and accidental diseases that were referred to as acute, epidemic.

These include intermittent fevers such as malaria, plasmodium vivax with fever every three days, plasmodium malaria, plasmodium falciparium which causes death by parasite emboli in the capillaries of the lung, intestine, liver and brain.

Military fever is an epidemic disease that causes a violent fever for two to four days but often of low morbidity; putrid fever, now called septicaemia, which often causes death; bluetongue, inflammation of all mucous membranes; or third party fevers, pleurisy, chest flow.

And we must also talk about smallpox[34], now "variole". This disease is characterized by the appearance on the face first, then on the body of red spots and then pustules. These scars leave marks that made people ugly (e. g. Mirabeau, a parliamentarian during the French Revolution).

In the past, this epidemic caused the deaths of 50 to 75% of those affected by it. When 300,000 men were lifted in 1793 in Auvergne, only 30 to 50% of the young unmarried recruits aged 18 to 25 who had been infected with smallpox had been cured. The cantons where many people emigrated as masons in the Lyonnais region, or in the Saône valley, had many young people who had contracted this disease. However, the young people of the canton of Biollet and Saint Priest of the fields where the people of the family tree studied lived had very few patients. Perhaps proof of a healthy lifestyle.

But there are not only diseases, there are also very difficult living conditions: even in the middle of the 19th century, children under the age of eight worked between 15 and 17 hours a day in factories, on farms they were needed to keep poultry and livestock.

They were put to work at the age of six or seven in 1860, as soon as the boys were vigorous, they would plough or direct the plough animals, hard work that prevented them from growing properly. All this was at the expense of education. Children went to school in winter to "get rid of" them because there was nothing to do.

The men in the family branch that migrated to Beaujolais are taller (over 1m70), perhaps proof that they are better nourished or that the diet in this more prosperous region is more balanced.

Even if the school were free, the child had to earn some profits to cover his expenses or simply because the family needed it. The child was confronted with the reality of life very early on.

---

34 All classes of society were affected by this disease

It should be noted, however, that schools until about 1880 were few in number, unheated, poorly equipped and often very far from where people lived, so that it sometimes took several hours on foot to get to this place for only 3 or 4 hours of basic education.

Family time is a rhythm that will return throughout the family tree and which, with each wave, will reactivate the same problem.

These trees do not contain this type of life programming other than the fact that there are few births in May and June, conceptions in September and October, many births in July and August, conceptions in November and December, and October, conceptions in February).

Weddings were mainly organized in February or in and out of winter, which explains the dates of births.

It can be seen that deaths occur mainly in the winter months.

These repetitions are not the work of a particular family but rather the habits and constraints of the agricultural and masonry trades.

Let us take again the final branch of the family tree, the branch of Beaujeu.

o 3- **Mathieu** *1833-1898* marié en 1859 avec Jeanne D. *1835-1899*
Fils d'Annet et d'Antoinette F. il part de Biollet entre 1851 et 1856 (il a à peu près 20 ans) pour Beaujeu. Il va vivre 65 ans (Jeanne sa femme mourra aussi à 65 ans) et il s'est marié à 26 ans. Maçon
Ils auront 7 enfants :
Il aura 29 ans à la mort de son père.
Les enfants 2, 3, 4, 6, 7 mourront très tôt
Il restera seulement 2 garçons : Jean-Marie et Jacques (10 ans plus jeune que Jean-Marie)

O 2- Pierre *1862-1868 (décès à 6 ans)*
o 3- Claudine *1864-1864 (décès à la naissance)*
o 4- Hippolyte *1865-1868 (décès à 3 ans)*
o 5- **Jacques** *1869- maçon, 1m74,* 5ème
régiment de cuirassiers. Il aura 29 ans à la mort de sont père (comme son père à la mort de son père) ; son degré d'instruction est 2. En 1898, 1901, 1909,1913 il aura fait quelques infractions comme violence, abattage d'arbre ..
Campagne contre l'Allemagne 1915-1916 réformé pour atrophie pupillaire d'origine traumatique. Certificat de bonne conduite
A habité à Villeurbanne (Rhône) à partir de 1916. Célibataire semble-t il. Il est peut-être décédé en 1917

o 6- Jeanne *1870-1875 décès à 5 ans*
o 7- Jeanne-Marie 1877-1877 décès naissance
o 1- **Jean-Marie** *1859-1905* &1883 **Benoite B**
1863- 1934 - Elle était aide de ménage.(* on reparlera de Benoite plus loin)
Maçon, 1m66. Service militaire au 134e régiment infanterie
son degré d'instruction est 3

Ils ont eu 8 enfants :

o 6- **Francoise** *1896-1898*
(décédé à 2 ans)
o 7- **Joseph** *?1900-1905 décédé 5 ans,*
l'année de la mort de son père
o 8- **Francois** *1901-*
o 1- **Jeanne-Francoise** *1884-1886*
(décédée à 4 ans)

o 2 - **Antoine** *1886-1919, maçon, 1m73*
guerre 14-18, prisonnier de guerre à St Hilaire le grand,
mort à Lyon en 1919 à 33 ans, quelques jours après son
retour
il était soutien de famille,
il avait 19 ans à la mort de son père
      o 3- **Jeanne** *1887-1910* mariée en 1905
      avec **Jean B** *1880-*
mariée à 18 ans, décédée à 23 ans à Villefranche sur Saône.
Mariage la même année que la mort de son père
en fin de la même année est décédé son frère Joseph
(* on reparlera de Jeanne plus loin)
      o **Jacques** *1891-1975* &1919 **Valentine D**
1898-1984 , décédé à 84 ans, marié à 28 ans, engagé volontaire à 18 ans dans les
cuirassiers à Lyon, ancien combattant, prisonnier de guerre en Allemagne, 1m71, Il
sera ferblantier à St Didier sur Beaujeu
il avait 14 ans à la mort de son père : ils auront 1 fils
      o **Gaston** 1920-1977 (mort à 57 ans)
      marié avec **Suzanne X,**
      ils auront 2 enfants
      o **Louis-Antoine** *1894-1940* , marié à
28 ans en 1922 avec **Jeanne R** *1896-1933* ; Jeanne mourra à 37 ans à Villefranche sur
Saône d'une péritonite ; 10 ans de mariage seulement
Ils auront un fils : **Lucien** 1924 marié en 1949 avec **Colette B** (ils auront 3 enfants)

It was Mathieu 1834-1898 mason who, born in Biollet, settled in Beaujeu (Rhône) where he married. Mathieu probably couldn't write. He married Jeanne, from a modest background (domestic) and orphaned by his father (owner/ farmer) at his marriage. They had 7 children.

The fact that they lived near a tannery in Beaujeu ("Paradise Bridge district"), which pollutes the water, can probably explain this very high mortality rate. Mathieu and Jeanne both died at 64 years of age a year later.

Jean-Marie 1859-1905 was a mason like his father. He died early at 45. He married Benoîte B. from modest means (a domestic helper), who died at the age of 71. She was orphaned by her mother at her wedding. They had 8 children.

Five died before the age of 5.

Antoine the elder brother returned to the 10th regiment of cuirassiers in 1907. He was 19 years old when his father died. Reformed as a family breadwinner, he was nevertheless recalled in 1914. Prisoner of war at St Hilaire le grand, he died in Lyon in 1919 at the age of 33 for mysterious reasons.

Jacques the second brother joined the army at the age of 18 in 1909, Louis-Antoine, the third son was 15 years old.

Louis-Antoine was 11 years old when his father died in 1905. That same year saw the marriage of her sister Jeanne (1 month after her father's death) and at the end of the year the death of her brother Joseph at the age of 5.

Three years later he also joined the army in the 10th regiment of cuirassiers in Lyon before leaving for Africa as Spahi two years later...

When Louis-Antoine married Jeanne R. in August 1922, he was 28 years old and orphaned by his father, just like Jeanne, whose father, grandfather, great-grandfather and uncles had died young.

Jeanne R. died in 1933 at the age of 33, leaving a son Lucien, born in 1924, orphaned by a mother at 9 and then by a father in 1940 at 16.

Louis-Antoine could have been a mason like his father and great-grandfather or a zinger later on like his brother Jacques.

When his father died, his mother found herself raising a family of 5 (4 after 1906) children. Living in a "place de l'église" apartment in Beaujeu, his resources were more than modest, his work as a household help and washerwoman was not enough to support the family properly. The marriage at the age of 18 of her daughter Jeanne (*see below) may be a result of this situation. His children nevertheless had an honourable education for the time.

The boys in this family were therefore unlikely ever to be teachers, engineers or doctors, their cultural capital was too weak. The army seemed to them to be the possible way out of their condition and into a certain social promotion, but perhaps they had no other choice.

At that time, social mobility was low, with notions of continuity and transmission embedded in the social structure (today children can follow a different trajectory from that of their parents much more easily, since society is much less rigid than at the beginning of the century).

A sick background can be cured simply by changing one's point of view. The army at that time could allow this break-up and act as a social elevator. Jacques and Louis-Antoine tried this path without knowing that two years later they were going to be thrown into the most deadly of wars.

The "family novel" since the arrival in Beaujeu was beginning to weigh a little heavy. For this sibling, everyone has had a different destiny, perhaps this is a new fact. Louis-Antoine's social trajectory allowed his descendants to envision and access a better future, which was the case.

Any member of a tree can be criticized a posteriori, but it is out of the question to judge, their behaviour is a reflection of a difficult time; there are indeed some family secrets that sneak in from generation to generation.

The observation of this reality confirms that individual destinies with their share of singularity are not independent of the social field in which they appear and evolve.

Remobilized in 1938 and knowing that he was seriously ill, Louis-Antoine enrolled his son in the Lorient Naval Academy. Lucien was 16 years old.

Since his birth he has followed his parents to different regions where his father, a gendarme, is assigned, then when his mother dies, he finds himself alone with his father.

At the age of 18 in 1942, he was sent to the Alger Navy unit in Senegal, Morocco, Mauritania and Madagascar. He left the French Navy in 1949 at the age of 25 (Louis-Antoine left the army to join the Gendarmerie in 1921 at the age of 27). Lucien left the Navy permanently (military periods) in 1965 at the age of 41 (Louis-Antoine was released from his duties in the Gendarmerie in 1939 at the age of 45).

We are witnessing an astonishing phenomenon of repetition of life scenarios.

The influence of other family trees......

Until now we have studied the elements of a family tree that can be summed up as a family name.

It should be remembered that a marriage is the junction of two family trees. The effects and traumas are not, of course, cumulative. There are power relations that come into play.

Thus Jean-Marie S. (1/12/1859-30/5/1905- died at 45 years old and Mathieu's son) married Benoite B* (she was 42 years old at the death of her husband)

*Benoite B. born on 23/08/1863, died at 71 on 12/04/1934

She married Jean-Marie S. at the age of 20 on 14/06/1883

Benoite's paternal family has lived in Beaujeu for a long time and the maternal family is from Saint Christophe, a commune north of Beaujeu on the Haut Clunisois plateau.

His father is a farmer in Beaujeu. It is indicated that her mother was a household helper and that her parents were homeowners.

His parents, married in 1862, had three children: Benoite was the eldest, then came in 1865 Rosalie (married to Claude C eleven years his eldest) and in 1868 Pierrette.

So Benoite got married in 1883

Two years earlier in 1881 his mother died, Benoite was 18, Rosalie 16 and Pierrette 13.

Benoite was a domestic worker in a baker's shop in the Church district of Beaujeu, her future husband lived in the nearby Quartier des Pères.

Pierrette B (Benoite's sister) had a natural daughter Louise (12/02/1891), at 23 years old, and married two years later with Pierre F (born in 1869 - tinsmith by profession) on 20/10/1893 (he will sign the death of Jean-Marie, Benoite's husband, his wife's sister)

It should be noted that on 17/2/1891, 5 days after Pierrette gave birth to Louise, Benoite will give birth to Jacques (who will be a tinsmith by profession like his uncle): the two sisters gave birth a few days later (they lived in the same neighbourhood, perhaps the same house).

Jean-Marie and Benoite were married in 1883; in the same year, Benoite's sister Rosalie died.

They settled in the same area as Pierrette (Benoite's sister), i. e. Quartier du Paradis in Beaujeu (about a hundred meters from the Quartier de l'Eglise)

In 1887 Jeanne their daughter was born.

In 1890 François Benoite's father died

In 1891, Louise, daughter of Pierrette, was born and Jacques, son of Benoite, was born.

That same year 1891, Jean-Marie's mother, Jeanne D., died in her turn

1893 on 14/9 marriage of Pierrette, Benoite's sister

1896 Birth of Françoise, daughter of Benoite and Jean-Marie
    in 1898, two years later, on 28/02/1898 Françoise's death, the same year as Mathieu Jean-Marie's father (Benoite's husband)

1901 Birth of Joseph on April 4, son of Benoite and Jean-Marie
    1905: this date is symbolic as the years 1891 or 1896, because the same year we witness the death of Jean-Marie (Benoite's husband), the death of Joseph his son, the marriage of his daughter Jeanne at the age

of 18 years with Jean Béranger (from Belleville) (who will marry again on November 3, 1911, 6 months after his wife's death)

Jeanne died in 1910.

But between 1905 and 1910, there was an event (ghost) for which there is no explanation.

What happened in Jeanne's life?

Indeed on January 30, 1907 she gave birth to a natural son, Henri S. in Lyon 2nd district, at 1 rue de la Charité (at the Hôpital de la Charité, which is a hospital for the poor people), she lived then at 21 rue Casimir Périer in Lyon 2nd district and was a day worker. (She conceived her son in May 1906: what happened between June 1905 and April 1906? She was no longer with her husband? She abandons her son who keeps his mother's last name)

She therefore abandons her son who is entrusted to host families.

RO ENTS	DATE des PLACEMENTS	NOM, PRÉNOMS ET PROFESSION des NOURRICES OU PATRONS	DOMICILE	DATE des RENTRÉES à l'hospice	OBSERVATIONS
	21. 2. 1907	Chanton Emile	Dornas (Ardèche)		
	24. 1. 1910	Charra Albert à Lacoud	Chirod (Ardèche)		H(+)/330
	25.3. 1911	Morel Pierre à Chauchon	Auge of Tresh...		550/455
	25.3. 12	-d-	-d-		800 - 667
	30.4.1912	Moulin Paul au bourg	Arches Dôme		464 - 864 au 2.7/12
	25-3. 13	-d-	-d-		905 - 455; 12-1.14
	25-3. 1914	Perrot Louis a Jullieu	Lyon (Dôme)		1000 - 275-5 ...
	25.3. 15	Chabot Antoine Fourille	Lyon (Dôme)		2000 - 1139 ...
	25.3.16	-d-	-d-		2600/1843 1...
	13.5.17	appelé au 170 Régt d'Infanterie à Die (armée du Rhin)			

In 1906, however, the records indicate that Jeanne lived in her mother's house in Beaujeu, Quartier du pont Paradis.

Antoine, Benoite's eldest son, lived not far from, rue de la République, he was a coachman

In the year of Henri's (Jeanne's son) birth in Lyon, Antoine, Jeanne's brother, joined the 10th regiment of cuirassiers in Lyon

In 1908, Antoine was discharged for "family head".

29 October 1909: Jacques his brother joined the 3rd regiment of cuirassiers in Lyon

November 14, 1910: Jeanne died at the age of 23 at the Beaujeu Hospital. The causes of his death are unknown. Jeanne must have been very sick and/or destitute.

In 1911 Benoite and his son Antoine lived in the Quartier de l'Eglise

In 1912 Louis-Antoine, Benoite's son joined the army, the 10th regiment of cuirassiers, then the 1st regiment of Moroccan spahis, then the 5th regiment of Algerian spahis.

In 1914, Antoine, living in the church square,"place de l'Eglise", was called back to the army

In 1914 Jacques, Benoite's son, was wounded and taken prisoner of war

In 1918 Antoine was also made a prisoner of war

In 1918 Louis-Antoine left for the Oriental army

In 1919, a few days after his repatriation and demobilization, Antoine died in Lyon 7th

That same year 1919, Jacques his brother married Valentine, a year later Gaston was born their only child.

In 1921 Benoite moved again and lives in "place de la grenette" in Beaujeu (near the Church)

In 1921 Louis-Antoine left the army and returned to the 7th Légion de gendarmerie on horseback

A year later, in 1922, Louis-Antoine married Jeanne R. (from Saint Didier sur Beaujeu and whose father was a sabot maker)

In 1924 Louis-Antoine and Jeanne R had one son (their only child) Lucien

In 1926 Jacques, Valentine (his wife) and Gaston (their son) lived in the upper part of the city:

Benoite lived in 1926 in the church district,"quartier de l'Eglise", in 1931 in the Place de l'Hôtel de Ville until his death in 1934

In 1933 Jeanne R., Louis-Antoine's wife, died at the age of 33 of an illness at the Villefranche sur Saône Hospital

In 1938 Louis-Antoine was recalled to the army and died in 1940

In 1940, Louis-Antoine's son entered the Lorient Navy School at the age of 16.

Conclusions

A family tree in a more general and complete aspect has several angles of vision. If we look at Jean-Marie's wife's family, we can still see repetitions of life scenarios.

There are similarities in the behaviours of the different members of this family.

Jean-Marie left his initial family group (due to a lack of living members in reality) to live with his wife Benoite's family members (they lived in the same neighbourhood Quartier du pont Paradis).

Benoite and his children lived in very close neighbourhoods in the centre of Beaujeu, so they saw each other frequently.

In addition to the various deaths that have occurred since 1905, the story of Jeanne, Benoite's daughter, has caused deep traumas. The death of Jean-Marie, Benoite's husband, the year of Jeanne's marriage, could have been a trigger for instability. All these facts may have caused the three sons' decisions to join the army. The army may have seemed to be a solution for getting out of a socially and psychologically difficult family environment.

Let us now consider the introduction of another family tree, that of Louis-Antoine's wife.

Louis-Antoine (son of Jean-Marie and Benoite) was married on August 5, 1922 in Saint Didier sur Beaujeu, commune of his wife Jeanne R.
He is 28 years old and she is 26 years old.
The previous year in 1921, he had become a mounted policeman at the 7th Gendarmerie Legion

Jeanne's family was quite wealthy for the time, her father was a clogmaker.
Louis-Antoine's brother had married in 1919 in Saint-Didier sur Beaujeu. So the families could get to know each other.

In the cemetery of Saint Didier sur Beaujeu next to the church is the family tomb of Jeanne R.'s family where they are buried:
-Jeanne R. married S. who died on May 2, 1933 at the age of 37
-Claude R. 1861-1939 - died at 78 years old - Jeanne's father
-Marie P. 1863-1949 widow of Claude R. 1863-1949- Jeanne's mother
-Joanny R. died on May 11, 1968 at 74 years old - Jeanne's brother
-Clotilde R. 1888-1973 (85 years old) - Jeanne's sister

In the same cemetery, we find the tomb of Jacques S., his wife Valentine and his son Gaston

At the Beaujeu cemetery, all that remains is the grave of Louise, the daughter of Pierrette, one of Benoite's sisters.
In the cemetery of the village of Fleurie we find the grave, in very good condition, of one of their cousin, Gabriel (1914-1983) and his parents Gabriel (1888) and Marie-Louise, who came from Biollet, Auvergne.
Of all the names mentioned in this document, these are the only tombs still visible.

The members of Jeanne R.'s family tree (Louis-Antoine's wife) also suffered from the many deaths.

These families all lived in the villages of the Haut-Clunisois region (on the plateau north of Beaujeu).

Jeanne R.'s parents were married on 06/09/1884 in a village named Tramayes. Her father Claude R (29/08/1861-1939) was born in Matour (Haut Clunisois), and was a clogmaker. Her mother Marie Antoinette P (31/03/1863-1949) was born in "Tramayes les sapins":

They will have 8 children but 4 will die before the age of 2 years old..:

- Marie-Claudine R 07/08/1886-18/11/1886 deceased at 3.5 months
- Claudine R 26/08/1887-18/11/1887 died at 3 months
- Clotilde R 17/11/1888- 16/04/1973 died at 85 in Lyon
- Frédéric R 17/07/1890- 28/05/1965 in Lyon 8th, 75 years old
- Jeanne R 31/07/1892- 15/11/1894 died at 2 years old
- Joanny R 29/07/1894- 11/05/1968 died at 74 years old in Beaujeu
- Jeanne R 14/07/1896- 02/05/1933 died at 37 years old
- Paul R 26/09/1899- 28/09/1899 died at 2 days

In addition to Jeanne R's death due to peritonitis, the other members lived for more than 75 years in good physical and moral health. An examination of the entire family tree going back to the 16th century shows that the families were owners, farmers, weavers, miller, carpenters, innkeepers... Life expectancy was, on the whole, quite high, even very high, since we observe ages regularly exceeding 85 years from the 15th century. Their level of education in the 19th century was good and it can be seen that there were fairly close family ties of solidarity.

Thus this marriage, through the arrival of this family tree, had a repairing effect on the Louis-Antoine tree. This trend was subsequently accentuated.

SAINT-DIDIER-SUR-BEAUJEU (Rhône) -- La Grande Rue

The army

The social elevator did not exist. To get out of their social condition, enlisting in the army could be one of the solutions.

Here is a short reminder:
Systematic conscription in France dates back to 1798. During the Empire, Napoleon introduced the random draw and defined the criteria for exemption from military service. Each canton had to provide a certain number of recruits. The prizes were drawn each year and young people who had a number above the required quota were exempted, as were married men, priests and anyone who could afford someone to replace them for 1500 to 1800 francs (which put a large amount of money into circulation[35]. There was also an increase in religious vocations and marriages between 18-year-olds. This was not the case for the men presented in the family tree studied.

In 1818, a new law[36] was defined, not very different from the previous one. The duration of military service was six years in 1818, eight years after 1824, seven years between 1855 and 1868, five years until 1889.

10% of men were involved in conscription, especially poor boys who were looking to earn some money.

Regarding the family tree used as an example, we do not know if any of its members have done military service. If so, this could explain in some cases the late marriages at 30 years of age and the financial difficulties encountered by the family.

---

35 Selon Louis Peygnaud, "Le bal des conscrits", le total des sommes dépasse 70 millions de francs-or
36 Celle du ministre de la guerre Laurent Gouvion-Saint-Cyr

Some farmers bought their sons back, not out of affection but because they could no longer farm their land.

Conscription was not considered a duty but a heavy tribute imposed by the State.

The substitution was abolished by the 1873 law, which also confirmed the duration of service at five years. At the same time, the government introduced a whole series of exemptions intended mainly for educated classes, students, teachers, priests, seminarians, eldest sons of large families or those whose fathers had died. Some sectors of public opinion advocated universal military service, in order to restore respect for authority and above all as a means of generalizing education.

But the upper classes did not like the idea of seeing their sons under the flags with the peasants' sons.

During this century there was no inclination of men to military service, and even a certain antipathy pronounced for service considered as a tax. To avoid it, there were numerous self-mutilations on the part of the conscripts.

Five years of service removed essential labour from the farm and fields, increased local wages, delayed marriages, and discouraged young people from settling in.

In 1889, the service was reduced to three years.

In 1905, the length of service was set at two years.

In 1913, it was again set at three years.

Institutionalized migration and the mixing involved in military service had begun to take place in the 1890s, while in its limited form conscription had had little effect on rural mentality.

Until 1889, returning soldiers were feared and held in suspicion because they had adopted foreign ways and bad habits so much so that they were forced to adopt the rules of the community and even to unlearn French[37].

---

37 A.M.Duchatellier "De la condition de fermier"

In the 1890s relations between the army and the country improved, the army becoming the school of the country, promoting literacy and the French language.

Recruitment was regional and the men served in local units. The army made young people lose the stereotypes of their countries, their suspicions and their backward opinions. So when they return to their village, they are francized enough to francize their friends by their influence. Local speech was quickly eroded.

The army's diet, despite its Spartacian character, far exceeded that of many households. The soup was good and abundant. The soldier's food, housing, bed, hygiene, clothing and situation was better than that of the rural working classes.

During the 1860s, the soldier's average daily ration was 1.4 kilos of food, while the national average was 1.2 kilos, a figure that included the large quantities of food consumed by the rich.

Mortality and disease rates were lower for soldiers than for civilians in the 20-27 age group. Let us keep in mind that the vast majority of soldiers came from the poorest classes.

In the army barracks the working day was much less than a day's work on a farm and they still had fresh meat twice a day. For many, the army was the best moment of their lives[38]. Thus men drank and ate like never before. It is therefore not surprising under these conditions that, knowing the living conditions of their native country, a good proportion of these peasant soldiers decided not to return to their villages.

At the end of the service, the men were looking for jobs as jacks, coachmen, or entered the gendarmerie, the water and forest service, public works, the post office or the railways, unless they re-engaged. The army became the cradle of small civil servants. The army had become an agent of emigration and civilization, an agent as powerful, in its own way, as schools.

---

38 Probablement grâce aux réformes de Hubert Lyautey

Concerning the family tree studied, men who married late did military service or joined the army.

The names are as follows:

Concerning the family tree studied, men who married late did military service or joined the army.

The names are as follows:

Gervais 1867 (brother of the previous one) was exempted because his brother was on the military service. He went to Fleurie in Beaujolais.

Jean 1867, military service from 1888 to 1891.

Jean-Julien born in 1868, 1m67, from 1889 (he was 21 years old) to 1892 in the 4th Zouaves Regiment

Jean born in 1871, 1m69, married in 1896 (he was 25 years old), in the military service of 1892 (21 years old) then demobilized as an elder widow, then remobilized in 1914, in the colonial infantry, demobilized in 1918, disabled at 10%.

Jean-Marie born in 1882, 1m65, to the 11th dragon regiment in 1903. Remobilized in 1914 to the 36th artillery regiment. Campaign against Germany. 20% pensioner for bronchitis.

Eugène-André, born in 1886, brother of Jean-Marie above, 1m68, 12th artillery battalion in 1907 (21 years) until 1909. Remobilized in 1914-1918, 10% disability for various fractures.

Félix-Gervais born in 1888, 1m71, incorporated in 1909 into the 16th infantry regiment. War 14-18. War cross.

Jean-Marie born in 1890, incorporated in 1911 into the 12th artillery regiment, war 14-18. Go to the nurses' section. Demobilized for rheumatism and arthritis.

Etienne-François was born in 1891, in 1912 in the artillery regiment. To the armies from 1914 to 1919.

Anne 1754-1810 daughter of Marien married a soldier

Jean 1907 joined the army in 1914 in the air force at Lyon-Bron

Pierre 1851 married at 27 (1878), enlisted in the 108th line in 1872, corporal in 1874, he was released in 1877 (5 years of service)

André 1873-1908 married at the age of 19 (1892). Incorporated in 1894 into the Artillery Regiment until 1897.

Marien 1792-1869 (from Condoleix) married at 34 years old

Henri-Amable 1893, veteran, corporal who died at the front

Gervais 1832-1883 married at 37 years of age

Gervais 1893 married at 43, enlisted in 1913, veteran in the infantry, wounded, citation, war cross, corporal

Francisque-Félix, born in 1897, incorporated into the colonial infantry, corporal, disability pension 10%.

Eugène-Léon born in 1899, paid to the colonial infantry regiment, died in 1924 at the age of 25.

Annet 1793 married at the age of 32

Jean-Marie was born in 1859 in Beaujeu, in the 134th infantry regiment from 1880 to 1885. He made a first period of practice in 1888 and a second period in 1892. He married in 1883 at the age of 24. It is Antoine's father, Jacques and Jean-Marie who follow:

Antoine 1886-1919 born in Beaujeu. In 1907 to the 10th regiment of cuirassiers. Demobilized breadwinner, remobilized during the war, prisoner of war in St Hilaire le grand (Marne). Died in 1919 in Lyon 7th district.

Jacques 1891-1975 born in Beaujeu. Volunteered at the age of 18 with the 3rd and 6th regiments of cuirassiers. Veteran: wounded in Fontaines les Thermes, prisoner of war, interned in Germany in "Alten Grabow" until 1919. Invalidity pension 10%.

Louis-Antoine 1894-1940 born in Beaujeu, 1m75. Volunteered at 18. At the 10th regiment of cuirassiers in Lyon then two years later at the 1st regiment of Moroccan spahis, cavalier, blacksmith, wounded in Morocco, passes to the 5th regiment of Algerian spahis, Verdun campaign, then fight in the Eastern army in Macedonia, Brigadier Maréchal, rehired until 1921. Mounted policeman at the 7th Legion of Mounted Police in 1921. He married in 1922. It occupies various casernements (Jura, Isère, Haute-Saône, Rhône, Somme,...). His son was born in 1924 and his wife died in 1933 of illness. Recalled to active duty in 1938, died of tuberculosis in 1940. Military medal, colonial medal with Moroccan clasp.

Lucien, Louis-Antoine's son born in 1924, at 16 years old, orphaned by both parents, returned to the military school in Lorient, Toulon and Algiers. Veteran, active from 1940-1949, with military periods until 1964. Military medal for the under 20-year-old combatants

What we can notice:

The men in this family tree have made a significant contribution to national service.

Those who did not do military service were exempted for breadwinner or eldest son of a widow.

The men who migrated permanently had served in the army.

Most of these men, in the 20 to 35 age group, fought in the First World War.

Their presence in the army, associated with their job as masons for the vast majority of them, had several effects:

of marriages later than average

premature deaths

orphaned children

These distances made it possible to see other people, another world, facilitating francization.

These situations naturally had an effect on their characters and behaviours in terms of autonomy, open-mindedness, probably having acquired a sense of discipline and authority,

To say that they were happy would be an untruth, these men suffered in silence, as did their wives and children.

The knowledge of a family tree with its names, first names, dates, ages, professions is not enough to understand what life was like for these people.

Let's try to describe them a little bit better.

They are Auvergne residents of the Combrailles region (between the south of Creuse and the Allier, east of Riom).
How were they dressed[39] and how did they live?

Around 1830, in the surroundings of Saint Bonnet near Riom, we still see old men dressed in a large white serge cape that goes down to mid-thigh and is pleated above the waist. This cape is always open from the front and shows the jacket in the same fabric with large white buttons. On the abdomen shines a large copper loop. Their tops are fixed above the knee. The legs are tightened in gaiters. They have long, hanging hair; in some they are curly. They have a round hat with wide wings, less wide than in the regions of Pionsat and Saint-Gervais where they reach imposing dimensions.

Women wear large blue wool dresses; they take great care to roll them up from behind to show the lower edge always lined. The sleeves hardly exceed the elbow. The dress is open on the chest and shows a very red shirt. The hairstyle is a very flat white cap, on which two wide bands of fine cloth, floating on the shoulders, depend. Over their headdress, many peasant women wear a straw hat with velvet to guarantee themselves from the sun. Against the rain, women wear a large disc of braided straw, attached to the head with a ribbon tied under the chin. As for the men, a large grey wool cloth that they squeeze around their necks with a string and which goes down to their heels, wrapping the whole body, serves as their coat....

---

39 B.Gonod : "La France, description, Puy de Dôme..." Publication Loriol

More than a century ago, child hygiene was very poor.

From 1822 to 1831, the total number of births in the department of Puy de Dôme was 165,422, and there were 51,517 deaths before the age of 10 (31%).

[40]*In the western mountains, the human physique, which was strong and robust, weakened significantly at the end of the 19th century. The food consists mainly of rye bread. We eat soup, often a porridge made with rye flour diluted in milk and cooked in the omelet-shaped pan. We drink water and sometimes whey. In some houses, bacon is eaten on Sundays. In the eastern mountains, the constitution is weaker, the country is less fertile, the dwellings more unhealthy, the food more unhealthy. Between these two regions and in the lowlands, the population is healthier. In Limagne, people are stronger since the marshes have been drained, but the population remains poor and food is insufficient.*

The men of the Combrailles region, who migrated as masons, probably lived better with a more adapted and varied diet (their size was also a little higher). We have no information on the quality of life of their women who stayed in the region.

Concerning emigration, a statistical table by Préfet Ramond, dated 26 January 1808, summarizes that in the district of Clermont-Ferrand, only two cantons have emigrants (bricklayer, pitsawyer, squarer, hemp combinator, chimney sweep, small merchant, weaver - there were 500 young people who engaged in begging, a very lucrative industry because they each earn an average of 200 francs).

In the Ambert district, there were 8500 emigrants, many of them children with very low salaries.

There are 4000 emigrants in the Issoire district,

In the Riom district (Saint Gervais, Pionsat, Pontaumur, Pontgibaud, Biollet) there were 2000 emigrants, mainly masons, they bring in an average of 180 francs each.

---

40 B.Gonod : "La France, description, Puy de Dôme..." Publication Loriol

In the Thiers district, between 400 and 2000 people emigrated (hawkers, cartwrights, bargemen), bringing in 100 francs.

In reality, all these figures are underestimated because many did not need administrative papers. These numbers varied from year to year[41].

The population movement over the past hundred years in the department of Puy de Dôme is as follows:

1789	491.566
1831	573.104
1876	570.207
1911	525.916
1936	486.103

These figures make it possible to express the extent of population movements and to situate in a community the situation of the people in the family tree taken as an example.

---

41 Rapport du préfet Ramond sur l'émigration saisonnière dans les départements du Puy de Dôme en 1808.

Concerning education:

Mathieu (1836-1898) could not sign his marriage certificate in 1859. His children later knew how to read and write correctly (level 3 education level in the second half of the century in Beaujeu[42]).

In the past there were very few schools in Auvergne like everywhere else. The schools, entrusted to religious teaching congregations, were attended by children of the urban bourgeoisie, but there were none in Combrailles. However, in some large cities there were some schools run by a priest or a lay teacher, appointed by the priest and under his authority. The sons of wealthy peasants, merchants and craftsmen learned first to spell, then to read and write at least his name, to sign deeds, a little to count in order to keep a book of accounts. For girls, knowing how to read and write was not an obligation, except perhaps for the nobility and the upper middle class. However, there are particularly educated women in Lozère in the 16th century, but they were probably of Protestant faith.

The signature at the bottom of the pages of deeds is a criterion of the level of education; we see few in Saint-Gervais but a little more in Pionsat for example. The presence of signatures on a marriage certificate provides information on the quality of the persons invited to the wedding. People took great pride in trying to sign and show their ability to trace, most often without tying them, the letters of their names. These acts show the degree of ignorance of the countryside in the 18th and 19th centuries in the Combrailles region, the region of our example.

The children had a sitting-board, a board, a goose feather more or less well cut. The book, which was generally religious, was on loan from the school. The punishments were numerous, for the chatter, passing through the picket in the corner, the donkey cap, the beating

---

42 Beaujeu à cette époque vivait une certaine prospérité économique avec la viticulture, les tanneries, les papéteries entre autres)

with a stick. Heating was provided by a chimney fire, but the rest of the room remained cold and humid. The children wrapped themselves in a thick pilgrimage, their feet in hooves wet by the journey.

The teacher's remuneration was variable, from 5 cents to learn to read, 10 cents to learn to read, write and a little bit count, to 20 to 30 cents if arithmetic and Latin are included. Four hours of classes per day (they started at 7 a.m.), about fifteen days of holidays in September. Old ladies taught young girls before the Revolution. Some school teachers asked for permission to teach girls in different times and in different rooms. Authorization was not always granted.

At that time there were only 3 or 4 schools for 40 parishes between Cher and Sioule, we are no longer surprised after these observations that at the bottom of the notarial or Catholic registers we find the sentence "and who declared that they could not sign; of this inquiry". In this region there was in fact only one school worthy of the name, that of the collège de Pionsat (northwest of Saint Gervais d'Auvergne)[43].

Under the influence of the writings of philosophers who eventually penetrated the less developed layers of the countryside, under the pressure of the events of the Revolution, thanks to the bold ideas of people like Condorcet, Lakanal, a popular movement will emerge in favour of creating schools for the people.

From the 26th "florial year II" {calendar of the French Revolution}, the commune of Saint Priest des Champs took a decision to engage as a teacher the citizen Jean Gidel from Pionsat.

Other municipalities will follow and appoint people as teachers. The law of 27 "Brumaire year II" {calendar of the French Revolution} had provided for one school for 2000 inhabitants so the districts are getting organized. Biollet 978 inhabitants joins Villossanges 1097 inhabitants. A jury is responsible for examining the candidates, focusing on civics and morality and the elements of the French language. Meeting these criteria, the candidates were elected. There are as many boys' schools as there are girls' schools. Despite good intentions, these

---

43 Bulletin n°12 de l'Association des anciens élèves maîtres de l'Ecole Normale d'instituteurs de Clermont, par M. Bachaud, professeur

schools were struggling to function, teachers were struggling to make a living from this profession, and students were not very present. The teachers in their dark and worn clothes were there to reconcile the ignorant masses with a new world, as spokesmen for the lights and the republican message. School rooms and buildings very often remained in a pitiful state. Dark, humid, crowded, the temperature of the bodies was used as a means of heating.

During the first half of the 19th century, the teacher could be a retired soldier, a field guard, the local barber, the innkeeper, or the slightly more educated son of a peasant and often knew nothing about the subject he was teaching.

In 1833, François Guizot's law laid the foundations for public education. At that time France had 31420 schools, attended by 1.2 million pupils, more or less credible figures

By 1848, the number of schools had doubled and the number of students tripled, in addition to which there were illegal, unofficial schools. But we must not exaggerate the effectiveness of teaching, the level was very low in the countryside.

In 1863, one-fifth of children between the ages of seven and thirteen had received no education at all. The 1868 law requires municipalities with more than 500 inhabitants to have a girls' school with a number of exceptions.

Despite all this, the illiteracy of conscripts was decreasing: the proportion of conscripts who could read rose from 14.3% in 1826 to 62% in 1875 in France, but on that date, 800,000 children out of a total of 4.5 million school-age still did not attend school.

The great change came in 1880 with the reforms introduced by Jules Ferry, helped by the huge expenses of the Freycinet plan: thousands of schools were created at the same time as roads, bridges and railways. But before teachers could take on the role of "missionaries", they had to take on this role: not only did they have to create effective teacher training colleges, but their salaries had to be increased very significantly[44].

Teachers joined the class of the notables, often became town hall secretaries, and took care of the administration.

One of the reasons for the slow progress in the fight against illiteracy was that many adults did not speak French but patois (in the homes they did not speak French because the grandmother did not speak it) one fifth of the population[45]. In some regions French was taught as a foreign language[46]. Generalized military service helped to spread the use of French and make its use more familiar, girls did not benefit from the "civilizing" and "linguistic" contributions of military service.

Another reason why the school was considered useless was that the teacher taught the metric system when people spoke in thumbscrews, thumbstrings, counted in francs while people counted in louis and écus, all said in patois[47].

At the end of the century another army was developing, that of private and public employees whose access was opened by the primary school certificate, a diploma as important if not more important than the First Communion.

Propaganda encouraged ambition, so many farmers wanted to stop being farmers and live something else. The state bureaucracy accelerated people's education because it was no longer reserved for a certain privileged class. The Third Republic made these posts accessible to the most modest.

Thus instruction brought civilization, new ways of life because schools also taught order, cleanliness, efficiency, success and culture. Schools, as a great agent of socialization, also taught great lessons in

---

44 Maitre débutant 700 francs par an en 1881, 900 francs entre 1897 et 1905, puis 1100 francs
45 Sept millions et demi de personnes, mais le nombre réel était probablement supérieur
46 "Tour de France" de Bruno 1877
47 Martin Nadaud "Mémoires de Léonard, ancien garçon maçon" 1912

morality centred on duty, effort, seriousness of intentions, patriotic feelings and patriotism.

From 1880 onwards, the classes were covered with maps of France. At the end of the century, children were taught that their first duty was to defend their country, and the army was valued. Teachers implanted love of the homeland, and at the same time provincialism was fought.

The school glorified work as a moral value but ignored work as a daily form of civilization, reinforcing the natural aversion to the hard work and thus facilitating emigration to the cities. Individuals, escaping the grip of old values, were oriented towards other beliefs

The 19th century is the century of a profound, progressive, total change. These evolutions must be taken into account in the analysis of a family tree. We then understand why people emigrated, went to the army, we understand their suffering and the questions they may have had.

Adriaen Van Ostade
(1610-1684)
"Le maître d'école"

Chapter 4

Historical traumas of a national population

"Everything passes, everything fail and nothing holds up"
Heraclid

"Everything will be forgotten and nothing will be repaired. The role of reparation (and by revenge and forgiveness) will be held by forgetting. No one will repair the wrongs committed, but the wrongs all the wrongs will be forgotten. "Milan Kundéra

"History is never the work of a single person, no one is its conductor or craftsman, no one shapes it because it is not man in the singular, who lives on earth, nor man and his enemy, it is men in their overflowing multiplicity. »
Hannah Arendt

Sociological researchers, anthropologists and health practitioners agree that: "Traumatic events of the past are important ingredients of our social heritage and continue to have an impact on the opportunities and limitations of the universe in which we live.

Images of traumatic events that have permeated the social memory of peoples eventually fade over time, "become stereotyped and selectively distorted and, as such, enter into the collective representation of the past that peoples pass on from generation to generation".

A person born in the twentieth century does not remember the suffering experienced by his ancestors; but he carries within him "images that are shaped by the memories transmitted by legions of men and women that we have never known and will never know". This person may be subject to secondary traumatic stress[48].

Secondary traumatic stress[49] refers to the behaviours and emotions generated in a relative of the actual trauma victim who became aware of the event: "For people who are close to a victim, being exposed to this knowledge can also be a confrontation with impotence and disruption.

It is the stress resulting from learning about the event or helping or attempting to help a person who is traumatized or suffering.

Thus, to fully understand this process, it is not necessary for the person to have witnessed the trauma, it is sufficient for them to have been informed. The trauma has become stratified and cumulative, affecting successive generations with their environments.

Psychiatrists, psychologists, anthropologists and social workers agree that experiences of violence and trauma resulting from massive and horrific deaths, coupled with the loss of everything that was safe and familiar, have profound influences on psychological functioning.

How to describe the intergenerational transmission of the historical trauma suffered by the "opening" towards the outside of the French countryside. Has there been any trauma and if so, what could have been the post-traumatic effects?

---

48 Les chercheurs utilisent divers termes pour expliquer le processus de transmission des souvenirs traumatisants. Miller, Stiff et Ellis (1988) l'appellent *contagion émotionnelle*. Dixon (1991) parle de *victimes périphériques*. McCaan et Pearlman (1990) examinent le traumatisme transmis par personne interposée et Danieli (1982) décrit les effets transgénérationnels du traumatisme. Parmi les autres concepts connexes, on retrouve celui de l'effet du survivant secondaire, l'effet d'entraînement et le traumatisme infectieux (Remer et Elliot, 1988). D'autres chercheurs établissent aussi une distinction entre le stress traumatique primaire et secondaire (Bolin, 1985).

49 D'après Figley et Kleber

It is curious to note that a range of disciplines, including history, anthropology, psychology, psychiatry, sociology and political science, are used to analyze the traumas of colonized peoples, but few studies are concerned with the traumas perceived by ethnic groups in our countryside.

Historical trauma is understood as a cluster of traumatic events. Hidden collective memories of this trauma, or collective amnesia, are passed down from generation to generation. The invasion of a region, subjugation, the imposition of a new language, the change of an account system, a currency, rulers, rape, can lead to profound disruptions in social functioning. The effects can be felt over many years, decades and even generations.

The link between peasants and their lands, their natural and spiritual environment, their social systems, their economic and religious practices is very important. Against the arrival of new ideas, it will be easy to understand that they sought to preserve the link that preserved their cultural and traditional values despite pressure from outside forces.

The peasants resisted for a very long time the assimilation of a central Parisian power while knowing very well that this cause was lost in advance. This resistance is not over, however, as some seek to maintain not only local traditions but also regional languages. As soon as a national identity is created, another battle is on the horizon in the face of globalization.

By relaxing the pressure, the State indirectly allows the formation of other economic, political and cultural areas.

The peasants are not cured but they are less visible because the countryside has desertified.

As they disappear, the villages see all the old ties disintegrate. The economic model replaces the collective model. The virtual image replaces the icon.

The demographic collapse of our countryside is causing a deep trauma, disrupting our collective unconscious.

Previously, a trauma was caused by war, famine, food deprivation, death of relatives, diseases, injustices, today it is more subtle, deeper; the legacy left to future generations will no longer be the same. This story has not yet been written and we can only postulate post-traumatic stress disorder; how to define the large number of mental disorders, suicides, alcoholism, drugs, madness, murders, attacks...boredom.

It is not only the event itself that causes the characteristic symptoms. The psychological atmosphere within a society or group of human beings is a factor that facilitates or hinders the process of dealing with difficult life events. A family environment has several circles, the village is part of one of them. A village had a spirit, it was structuring. A city is more about individualism and clanism. The psychological atmosphere is not only distorted but also unhealthy. Psychologists and social workers focus their attention on this slow and continuous dislocation with multiple roots, but the work is immense and unfathomable.

It will take time to accept that these traumatic situations can produce persistent personality changes and can be cured.

When a trauma is not taken into account, often because it is not visible, or perceived as such, the trauma in question is transmitted from one generation to the next.

Trauma and its repercussions generally go back further than is usually recognized.

The experience of historical trauma and intragenerational grief can be described as psychological baggage passed on from parents to children along with the trauma and grief experienced in the life of any individual. The hypothesis is that the residuals of traumatic, historical and unresolved experiences and generational or unresolved grief are not only transmitted from generation to generation, but are continuously acted upon and recreated in contemporary culture.

Contagions are caused by emigration and the movement of individuals such as plagues. These devastated the countryside and Europe for centuries, killing half the population in the 15th century[50].

Unfortunately, the people were illiterate and so most people did not write letters, did not keep a diary, these documents that would help us to understand the extent of the suffering and grief they were experiencing. It is therefore impossible to read how people could have organized themselves, helped each other despite the fear and general confusion. It is therefore difficult now to feel empathy in the face of misfortunes that are hard to imagine now. However, many letters and newspapers have been preserved during the periods of calamities that decimated European populations for at least 400 years, but these testimonies written by educated people come from a wealthy class, and in fact express partially and clumsily, confusingly, the misfortunes of the people and the people of the terroirs.

In Europe, the Black Death has finally been recovered through spiritual and economic processes and social adaptation. For some, the return to normal activities was relatively simple.
Many large and small cities have discovered that they can survive the occasional loss of large portions of their population. The population was quickly replaced by births and immigration.

The men of the Middle Ages were therefore very far from being able to read and write. But their churches and governments kept historical records, so that even in times of crisis, their deep cultural roots were not destroyed or fragmented.

Medieval Europe had experienced social, moral and spiritual disintegration as a result of the trauma caused by the plague of the

---

50 L'arrivée des Européens en Amériques, pendant plus de quatre cents ans, a tué jusqu'à 90 pour 100 de la population indigène continentale et traumatisant les peuples autochtones sur les plans physique, spirituel, affectif et psychique en leur infligeant un deuil profond et non résolu.

bubonic plague suffered for hundreds of years. Nevertheless, once the crisis ended, Europeans returned to their "roots" as their cultural memory had remained intact. In a way, "they knew who they were" and preserving their identity helped the recovery process.

During the 30-40 year intervals between the great afflictions, medieval Europe was able to gradually rebuild the social order and the population was able to renew itself. The lesson to be learned is that when traumatic events cease for a fairly long period of time (at least 40 years), socio-cultural reconstruction and healing can not only begin, but will do so, when this period is too short, in the order of ten years, this reconstruction is impossible.

The European continent thus suffered repeated attacks from the bubonic plague and other similar plagues from 1333 until at least 1720, when the plague arrived in Marseille from Central Asia.

Throughout the history of humanity, death has struck relentlessly, for as long as four hundred years. The Black Death in Europe was omnipresent. Epidemics were everywhere, striking at random, unlike wars and persecutions, which tend to be limited to a certain place or populations.

Plague and smallpox raged everywhere and struck blindly, regardless of age, social class, country or religion.
For 400 years, Europe has faced a "biological warfare";
In this war "smallpox was the captain of the soldiers of death in this war, typhoid fever the lieutenant, and measles the second lieutenant". A very efficient small army.

The disease was often accompanied by famine. As there was no one left to cultivate, trade, hunt, prepare food, reserves decreased rapidly, food flows were unstructured. Sick people whose immune systems were already seriously compromised did not have the strength to overcome hunger.

When such a large population suffers such significant losses and a balanced epidemiological, nutritional and reproductive system is not immediately restored, the situation exceeds the tolerance limits of that population: that is, the cumulative effect of multiple stressors over a short period of time threatens a group, and may either die out or cease to exist as a distinct cultural unit.

Medieval Europe also experienced social, moral and spiritual collapse resulting from the trauma of the Black Death between 1349 and 1351 and successive pandemics that raged across the continent at least until 1720, and then medieval Europe witnessed the reconstruction of the social order and population.

During the Black Death epidemic, then again during the War of 1914-1918, the immense loss of human lives created a psycho-physical shock.

Each time, it took time for the vitality and initiative of the survivors to return. And this would eventually happen when there was enough time between the initial traumatic event and the new traumas. In each case, the textures of society were modified by events; new openings were created and old ones closed; members of the old nobility died and new ones replaced them; chivalry and courtesy in their original form vanished; manners became crude and frustrated; and the refinement in clothing disappeared.

In other words, people were concussed and adopted attitudes from which they could not emerge for many years.

The effort to survive, generation after generation, in the face of physical danger contributed to psychological misadaptation and social pathologies, such as suicide, violence and alcohol abuse. Survival of the mind and body, in the individual and social sense, under conditions of excessive and abnormal pressure and deprivation, requires optimal adaptation responses. But many people, when they find themselves under siege, simply cannot do it.

the European history of diseases and epidemics provides us with information on the effects and transmission of unresolved trauma and grief. These effects are determined on different incidence domains such as the physical one for infectious diseases that have decimated populations in a high percentage without understanding the post-traumatic stress syndromes that this may have caused, the economic one because the diseases have caused emigration, destructured the internal functioning of a village and modified lifestyles, the modification of the belief system by denaturing theological foundations in favour of a social class.

The generational mourning of the First World War is not over; this continuous transmission of deeply buried emotions to successive descendants serves as a link with the past and reinforces a chronic sadness that unites a people. This unresolved grief remains both historical and contemporary; it is generational, intergenerational or multigenerational grief.

Traumatic events often have devastating and large-scale impacts on the health and stability of the nation and community. The 1940 war could be a result of this trauma. It is equally important to consider that the meaning of any traumatic event is a complex interaction between the event itself and the past, present and anticipated future of the person, and of a society.

For decades, all village communities have been traumatized by the many deaths caused by the disease, premature deaths, forced migration, loss of economic self-sufficiency, loss of language, changes in economic and political structures.

Farmers were separated from their lands especially at the end of the 19th century, lands that have always made a lot of sense to them; this separation has affected them in their existence and in their social constitution to this day.

Urban life codes have disrupted families, altered gender roles and weakened their cultural values.

Farmers and villagers in general lived within a complex socio-economic regime based on cooperation, the village was responsible for raising orphans, in the third circle, after parents and family.

Cities have introduced strong status distinctions, relegating peasants to subordinate roles, locking them in factories or mines. Visible inequalities and marked differentiation of social classes have been introduced.

The beginning of the 20th century, before the First World War and especially after, saw the destruction of ancestral community life and the modification of usual social contacts.

We have seen the cultural dispossession of land for national harmonization purposes, the marginalization of peasants, because their social identity has been significantly weakened and impoverished; any perception they had about their ability to control their lives has been diminished and considerably atrophied.

Farmers today see their jobs devalued, they themselves have difficulty living financially, the agricultural space is shrinking in favour of the forests that cover the landscape. Workers, most often the sons of farmers, have difficulty integrating into the urban environment and are even rejected on the outskirts of cities. The social elevator is still difficult for them to access.

Political centralism has led to the destruction of the cultural autonomy and identity of the terroirs, leading to changes in the psychological constitution of this mosaic of people.

What was inflicted on men during the First World War has all the characteristics of genocide and, as such, has caused trauma not only to survivors but also to their children and grandchildren. This complex post-traumatic stress disorder has become deeply rooted in the French people.

These events seem to have created a sense of fatalism and passivity that prevented the nation from having a clear vision of the world between the two wars and this led to a new war in which the people did not want to participate.

The nation has a legacy that is difficult to manage; there is no one to remember these events, but the "malaise" is perpetuated, the grief is permanent.

After 1918, France changed a balance that had already been damaged by the many epidemics because entire groups of individuals had been decimated by the epidemics, thus promoting the disintegration of communities.

The loss of a significant number of members of a village community has led to a change in authority roles and has changed existing social structures.

In the countryside, culture is oral, we only know what we can remember; in a village, memories are also private and collective.

The images of the dead have permeated the collective unconscious and constitute the core of traumatic memory. This nucleus is imbued with sadness, full of loss, heavy with grief.

Psychologists recognize that severe stress, caused by a traumatic event (military combat or other disaster) can be a predisposing factor for a personality disorder. Dissociated states can also occur in people who have been subjected to prolonged periods of intense persuasion such as brainwashing, or indoctrination, during captivity. It is therefore not surprising to see the importance that communist and fascist ideas and regimes had on people's minds after the First World War.

When loss is converted into absence, one finds oneself faced with the impasse of infinite melancholy; this impossible mourning has made the bedrock of doctrines. The entire nation has lost the sense of control over its own psychological resources. France lost its way in 1940.

There are many consequences to post-traumatic stress disorder experienced at the community level.

Survivors of the First World War carried with them constant images of death and atrocities. Some of these men described these images as films unfolding in their heads, others lost the memory of events, too many things were mixing in their brains. They find themselves with nothing and then all of a sudden all the memories come back at the same time, and that's too much. Many preferred not to say anything for fear of being misunderstood or not believed.

But recurring memories of the traumas experienced by members of a society eventually become part of a group's social narrative and will be passed on to future generations. These memories are incorporated into cultural collections of symbols and meanings, rituals and ceremonies, the group's common cultural memory and role models. This is what we are experiencing a century later.

Adults who are constantly reliving horrible experiences in their minds and behaviours will be less able to assume their parental and social obligations. Some will be unable to fully assume them. Relationships between people will be disrupted, marriages will break down and children will suffer. Some will be unable to express love or tenderness, being stunned themselves, they will raise children who will in turn be stunned and anesthetized and unable to express their emotions. This is one of the results of this war.

"The combined effect of many incidents of emotional abuse can lead to similar symptoms of repressed emotions, torpor and irrational thoughts that are triggered by unresolved problems and the loss of inherent identity. Those affected will remain insensitive to the outside world. They will perceive this world as hostile and feel that they have no control over it. They will feel alienated, detached, lonely and lonely. They will pass on their loneliness and alienation to their children who, in turn, will become lonely and desperate. Their bodies will be the only thing they can control and, even then, this sense of control will be very

fragile given the experiences they have had themselves in their lives. They will begin to use violence against their own bodies; they will drink until they are destroyed, they will breathe glue and gasoline, they will cut their arms off and go so far as to kill themselves. They will be unable to love.

Their inability will make them angry and they will start hitting and raping their wives and children, and inflicting the same fate on each other. Their children will not feel like they are reliving the past of their parents, grandparents and great-grandparents, they will ignore it. For them, terror will occur here and now. »

Here is a consequence that is never taken into account as a factor of explanation.

"Combining extreme violence with technological innovation, the 1914-1918 war traumatized the fighters. Shocking and unpublished documents make the voice of those who passed from the front line to the asylum heard. From the time of general mobilization and the first battles, the 1914 war, which no one anticipated would last until 1918, imposed a pace and violence for which no one was prepared.

And it started in the first month of August, the men were not prepared, did they at least know how to use their weapons? Psychiatry and military medicine were caught off guard. From the troopman to the officer, thousands of them suffered from behavioural disorders that could neither be treated nor described.

Gradually, however, a reflection on war neuroses and war traumas developed. But it was "forgotten", repressed, in the 1920s and 1930s, just as those who had gone mad as a result of the war, without necessarily having a visible wound, were marginalized and neglected[51]".

This war was not socially "just"; the men in the countryside were in poor health, fifty percent could have been exempted because of bone, lung and heart weakness. But they were sent to the front line in the infantry, many spoke only their local dialect. The rich, the intellectual

---

51Du front à l'asile, 1914-1918. Stéphane Tison, Hervé Guillemain. Alma éditeur, septembre 2014

professions, civil servants and the like were either reformed, dispensed or sent to support regiments behind the front, unless they were volunteers (and there were many of them). However, it was necessary to preserve the nation's "living" forces.

The First World War was not only fought in the trenches, but also in villages, factories and mines. Between the front and the rear, two different memories were set up. The true stories, overwhelming in their simplicity and sobriety, of these men and women, show the magnitude of the challenge faced by psychiatry, and the intellectual revolution that took several decades to come to fruition.

Today, Western opinion views the Great War mainly as an unnecessary "butchery" and a suicide of Europe. This vision is the result of a reconstruction of memory that is far removed from what the actors and witnesses to the conflict may have felt. The temporal context must be taken into account. In 1914, the major European powers entered the war, each being convinced that the other was the aggressor and that the war would necessarily be short. In each camp, the populations are all the more united and inclined to go to war because they believe that the conflict will be brief. In the cities men were better informed but in the countryside, for many this war will be their first trip out of their region.

To summarize and synthesize it, psychotrauma can be defined as the set of immediate, post-immediate and chronic psychological disorders that develop in a person after a traumatic event that has threatened their physical and/or psychological integrity.

"These disorders can last for months, years or even a lifetime in the absence of care, they cause great moral suffering linked to reminiscences (traumatic memory) with the implementation of avoidance behaviours (to escape them: phobias, withdrawal), hypervigilance behaviours to try to control them and dissociative behaviours to try to treat them.

"Associated mental disorders, often at the forefront, are mood disorders, anxiety disorders, personality disorders, self-injurious behaviour disorders, addictive disorders, conduct disorders, eating disorders, sleep disorders, sexual disorders.

After the armistice, out of more than 8 million French soldiers mobilized, 1.3 million died and about 3 million were injured. A very large number of them can definitely no longer work, 100,000 are severely disabled with a recognized disability rate of 85%.

Unlike the physically wounded, there is little consideration for the mentally injured; they receive little or no pensions, and are not entitled to free care. Yet the psychically traumatized are part of the huge cohort of war invalids, but the lack of warrior nobility of this type of pathology, new for the time, and the nature of the disorders presented by soldiers did not lend themselves well to the creation of influential associations such as the "broken jaws".

Thus, in the absence of a systematic count, the total number of war insane persons is difficult to estimate, but there were thousands. Many were considered "living dead" because their lives had become disconnected from reality, with no possibility of family or professional reintegration[52].

Neuropsychological war traumas had never reached the peak that will be observed during the First World War[53].

The war neuropsychiatrists of the time were confronted with many pathologies of such a new kind that they had a permanent suspicion of simulation. The debates between specialists were so strong that this will lead to therapeutic abuses[54] and excesses of military justice, which will not hesitate to shoot a number of soldiers.

The medical and military wanderings around these psychoneuroses, while they made it possible to authenticate the traumatic shock of war, led to the death of many men.

---

52 Journal des mutilés, réformés et blessés de guerre.
53 « La folie au front » Laurent Tatu, Julien Bogousslavsky, 2012, Editions Imago,
54 Comme la psychothérapie électrique

Combat-related nervous disorders had begun to be studied during the Napoleonic wars under the name of "ball and chain wind". Then during the American Civil War from 1861 to 1865, the Crimean War, the Franco-Prussian War of 1870, the Boer War of 1899-1902, the Russo-Japanese War of 1904-1905, the Balkan Wars of 1912-1913. Despite this, the army's health services did not take the real extent of these pathologies, so that war doctors, as early as 1914, found themselves confronted with soldiers suffering from psychological trauma and suffering from new or at least poorly known clinical conditions. The new syndromes divide neuropsychiatrists as to the real responsibility for the war. Some see the effect of the violence of the fighting as the main cause, others mention the explosion of ammunition, extreme living conditions on the forehead, the emotion created by the horror vision of death, and others will finally speak of conscious or unconscious simulation based on the fact that there was no visible wound[55].

The latter case gave rise to debate, allowing medical-military collusion to take hold to the detriment of the soldiers. This complicity of doctors with the military authorities was done under the benevolent gaze of learned societies. The medical abuses that have been followed seem to be a taboo subject[56], if not ignored. This question was belatedly revealed because it overlaps with the question of the soldiers shot; thus, soldiers whose psychological disorders were not detected were condemned and shot. The opinion of neurologists and psychiatrists, strongly involved in experimental drifts, played an important role in the decision. The Health Service, already involved in the misinformation on the safety of firearm injuries, did not anticipate issues related to neuropsychiatric disorders either.

Battlefield doctors are regularly confronted with soldiers who have suffered psychological trauma during the war, but are often helpless in the face of these particular pathologies that they do not control. Very

---

55 L'autopsie de soldats victimes de ces syndromes sans plaies extérieures a permis de découvrir des hémorragies diffuses dans différents viscères et dans le système nerveux.
56 Sujet qui implique des grands noms de la médecine

early on, these neurological wounded and psychically traumatized people very quickly cluttered the hospitals in the back. Centres are being established quickly in the rest of the country, but recruiting medical staff is difficult, people are not trained and the number of beds is insufficient.

In 1915, the centres were overwhelmed by the influx of patients. Care is minimal, the patients are sorted and the vast majority of soldiers are sent back to the front. The others are treated with psychotherapy, electricity and cold shower. Despite the importance of the patients, doctors[57] continue to put the number of war psychoneurotic patients into perspective. Despite everything, research on this subject is increasing in number, the involvement of civilian and university doctors is total without leading to a reasoned medical attitude.

As the months go by, after debates on terminological problems, three main mechanisms are defined to explain the appearance of disorders: concussion, resulting from undetectable organic lesions of the nervous system, emotion experienced on the battlefield which can trigger disorders through sensory means such as the vision of horrors or olfaction (smells of corpses) and finally the mechanisms of suggestion and self-suggestion placed in the context of hysteria.

Nevertheless, some doctors question the soldier's willingness to heal or consider that war is a sign of a congenital defect or predisposition, at best the soldier would simply suffer from overwork, physical fatigue, or even hypnotism in battle[58]. However, there are very many soldiers suffering from more or less acute mental disorders[59] as

---

57 Revues médicales spécialisées comme la Revue neurologique, les Annales médico-psychologiques

58 Gaston Milian « L,hypnose des batailles », Paris médical,1915

59 Celine wounded on October 24, 1914 in the Poelkapelle region of Belgium developed psychological disorders of war: overexcitement, complete sleep deprivation

reported in several literary works[60]. There are thousands of soldiers who committed suicide, usually on leave or during hospitalization[61].

Faced with the enormous human reservoir of patients with neuropsychic disorders concentrated in specialized centres, many neuropsychiatrists believed they were authorized to practice experimental medicine[62]. They did not hesitate to modify existing therapies such as electrotherapy to make them aggressive or painful. One of the goals mentioned was to rebuild the soldiers through intensive re-education to send them back to the front as quickly as possible, to avoid paying pensions and to save money in general. One can only notice the contrast between these doctors where pathetic and grotesque intertwine and the soldiers who, as Celine said, tried to hide their fear of the fighting and the front under the guise of primary patriotism.

On the battlefield, the inappropriate behaviour of neuropsychic traumas led soldiers to commit military crimes[63] and the fear of simulation prompted many doctors to send many patients to the war council[64]. In their defence, it must be said that the military hierarchy, fearing an epidemic spread of simulation on the front, exerted strong pressure on the medical profession. This did not prevent the phenomenon of voluntary mutilation by deceit from increasing, but on the medical level the problem of mutilation overlaps with that of war psychoneurotic diseases. Many such cases will be severely judged[65].

At the end of the war, the soldiers returned home with traumas and were not treated. The emotions experienced by all on the battlefield as a

---

60 « Ceux de 14 » Maurice Genevois, « « Le grand troupeau » Jean Giono
61 Denis Rolland « Le suicide aux armées en 1914-1918 »
62 Les publications, et conférences furent nombreuses
63 « Carnets de guerre » Louis Barthas, caporal au 280e régiment d'infanterie
64 L'état de siège du 2 août 1914 confie en matière de justice des pouvoirs exceptionnels à l'armée qui peut même juger des civils. En 1916 plusieurs lois modifient le fonctionnement de la justice et l'état de siège est levé
65 Roland Dorgelès « Les croix de bois », Marcel Proust « A l'ombre des jeunes filles en fleurs »

result of fear and horror visions are important elements in the genesis of war psychoneurosis. These men were doubly responsible for an emotional syndrome and a concussion syndrome. They have lived with these two physical and moral shocks and have shared them with their immediate environment consciously or unconsciously. These men, mainly from the campaigns that were put on the front lines, served as guinea pigs for people who had only deep contempt for them.

After the signing of the first peace treaty, there were the returns; the return of the soldiers, who a few days earlier were still fighting on the front line and could no longer stand it, the return of the internees in general in 1919, the prisoners held in Germany from their captivity and finally the return of the displaced civilian refugees.

There is also another return, that of a return to daily life. This "post-war" period will be perceived and managed differently depending on whether you are a man or a woman, a fighter or not. Each time they are complex situations that are difficult to manage. The soldier's return to his home did not necessarily go as well as he had anticipated. Modesty and trauma hide many secrets that have remained in the privacy of families.

Not all soldiers return to their homes at the same time. Some have already returned, due to injuries or illnesses they have suffered. But not all of them have resumed their activities, they have been sent to work in arms factories or mines. Others were definitively demobilized in 1919 and were able to reunite with their families, whom they had not seen for four years.

The professional soldiers will only have simple permissions for the end of the year holidays, and those of the Oriental army will not return for a long time.

The first moments of reunion were undoubtedly joyful but to varying degrees; there was the happiness of the end of the war, that of finding the person alive, but there was also a feeling of sadness that a family member did not return, joy gave way to grief, doubt, hope, misunderstanding and anger.

There are returns where soldiers discover their children they have never known because they were at the front when they were born. There are also sad days after victory when soldiers rushing home learn of the death of their wives, children, or family members.

Other returns were synonymous with disappointments: the discovery of extramarital affairs and adulterous children. Under these circumstances, veterans obtain facilities for divorce, but divorce was neither an easy thing nor a socially accepted act in early 20th century society.

All this left painful consequences and, for soldiers who had spent many months at the front, the post-war daily life will also be made of nightmares, reminiscences and serious physical and moral consequences due to the war.

Often there is a great silence about what happened "there". Sometimes out of modesty or to protect loved ones. Nor is it the kind of subject that can be easily discussed with those who have not experienced this type of event.

It is also often due to trauma and fear of not being able to control their emotions. A lead cap covers the memory of the old hairy man and his memories of war. Veterans' societies and fraternal groups will act as psychoanalysts. Those who could write had recorded every detail of this war in notebooks that they never showed. It is only much later that these war experiences will sometimes be shared, with its share of imagination.

For widows and war orphans, soldiers or civilians, there is no direct account and they live in the constant memory of the absent. It will become an obsession for some until their death, knowing that many of the soldiers killed had no graves.

The process of obtaining pensions and rebates takes up days, months and years. The State is fussy when it comes to paying or awarding disability pensions corresponding to the damage suffered. A real "paperwork" war is starting, especially for those with a low level of education, i.e. the majority of them, not to mention those who still speak only their local dialect.

The letters follow one another and all look alike: the complaint of the administration's slowness in handling their case and the feeling of having given so much for the country and having to wait so long to obtain rights. Teachers, among others, are mobilizing to help these veterans because the difficulty is so great.

In addition to these procedures, it is also necessary to follow the requests for decorations, accompanied by the soldier's often brief account and his war journey, especially if he has been taken prisoner. He will then be asked for details of his capture, testimonies from other soldiers or superiors present during his capture. These steps are tiring and weigh on the daily lives of families.

For the soldiers who returned disabled from the front, another life began with care, rehabilitation and revalidation. This new life began for many even before the end of the war.

Institutions for the disabled and war invalids draw up tables on the possibilities of reclassification according to disabilities; civil servant positions are created especially for them but many former farmers, these men from the terroirs, cannot work.

For the other war invalids, mainly those in the cities, professional rehabilitation workshops are being set up, with varying degrees of success, but this will not erase the consequences.

The elders of the Great War did not form a uniform social group, some preferred to distance themselves from the events of 14-18 and their subsequent lives, others chose to invest in associations of elders but above all they did not experience the same war: there were those at the front, the infantry and artillery regiments and those at the rear, in the administration and support units. Disabilities indelibly mark the veteran in his social life. But little by little, the general enthusiasm that had followed the war years faded. Time is working and at the end of the 1920s there was a rejection for the military thing, even a strong anti-militarist feeling.

Many die as a result of their disability or from conditions caught in the trenches. Later, another war would bring its share of pain and casualties, and the victims of the Great War would be somewhat erased.

The combatants' journeys, as varied as they were, were strewn with personal, administrative and ideological obstacles and some remained deeply resentful for the rest of their lives. This is the beginning of a transgenerational trauma.

The prisoners, soldiers, returned to France after the armistice, in droves, there was no one to welcome them. Yet among them are the sick and very weakened men.

The return of men will pose many logistical or moral problems, but in this year 1918, joy prevails first and foremost. The happiness of finding one's own and being free. Problems will then arise: they will be private, collective or institutional.

From the point of view of social psychology, the soldier was caught in the mass, drowned and became part of it at the cost of a loss of his autonomy and sense of responsibility.

This collective life has transformed these men from a state of isolated individual to a state of collective individual, placing them in a state of hypnosis; this state constitutes an essential motor for the modelling of behaviours. For the army, it was necessary to act quickly, the first month of the war in August was very deadly. Emotions and feelings had to spread very quickly within the troops to give more cohesion. The soldiers therefore passed very quickly twice through two social systems organized but differently. This was enough to shape irrational and uncontrollable behaviour later on. Social roles have been modified.

This war by its scale has contributed to changes in mindset, especially on the part of soldiers from rural France. The values and norms shared by the group, which a regiment forms, have changed their knowledge and practices, that is, their culture.

It is from this new social matrix that they will now organize their lives and relationships. This common culture will now play a role in integrating the terroirs within the French nation. The patois will disappear quickly, geographical mobility will be stronger and accepted, claims will be uncomplicated.

Women have worked in the fields, in factories, they have become independent, their eyes turn to the city, its way of life, fashion, a new food, a new light.

Man has lost his role as dominant leader, he will have to establish other modes of communication, relationships, two inseparable processes.

As soon as the war ends, people find themselves subject to different forms of social influence that will be very important. All compliance processes will be tested; individuals will change their beliefs and behaviour to other systems such as communism or fascism, a doctrine that includes both identification with ideas, with leaders, and their batches of followers and submitters.

Thus the soldier's topological space upon his return from the war has changed profoundly and he has had to adapt to another representation of the world.

This war has therefore upset all the frames of reference.

Chapter 5

The genosociogram

The transgenerational is what passes between generations in a fairly clear way, such as the passion for a profession, political ideas, ways, an art of living, a language.

The transgenerational is a current that flows through us, not visible, nestled in our unconscious and that indirectly conditions our behaviour.

We are complex because our inherited situations are complex.

By carrying out our genosociogram, we will not solve all the questions we may ask ourselves, but simply question ourselves and help us to pose the problems in a more formal way.

The American psychiatrist Ivan Boszormenyi-Nagy, asks four questions about family rules.

What would be the answers for the case studied?

"What are the rules in this family? ": the chosen first names, i. e. {Gervais, Annet, Marien, Antoine... } are accompanied by a family mission: these names are old, and linked to a family loyalty that will be interrupted as soon as one of its members migrates to another region.

"Who develops them? "he is the head of the family, the bearer of the family name. We will find first names from the wife's family at the end of the 19th and in the 20th century.

"Who transmits the rules? "Men married late and died early. The children were raised in a family circle extended to uncles, aunts, cousins, and grandparents. The community rules are those of the hamlets (a few families).

"Who says the rules? "the transmission is oral. Mothers have a very important role to play as men are often away from home for long months. In addition, mothers became widows at an early age.

We know almost nothing about our family history and the further up the tree we go, the more important the holes and omissions are, but that's also what makes them interesting.

The rules and their evolution depend on the norms and psychology of the time. We must therefore not project our ways of thinking onto another era.

To study your family tree is also to revive the dead, to understand what their sufferings and difficulties were, to establish links with our ghosts.

To improve our knowledge of each of our ancestors, it is interesting to try to build what is called the "social atom". This graph highlights the elements that are important to this person: human beings, animals, objects, events, plants, places, objects, historical, political or literary figures.

It is difficult to make the social atom of someone who has been dead for a long time but given the evidence we have we will try this experiment on 3 people.

This exercise will also make it possible to distinguish between them and to show how their concerns have evolved over time.

We will study in this way:

- Marien 1723-1780
- Mathieu 1834-1898
- Louis-Antoine 1894-1940

(recalls Louis-Antoine knew his father for 11 years, and his grandfather for 4 years)

► Marien 1723-1780

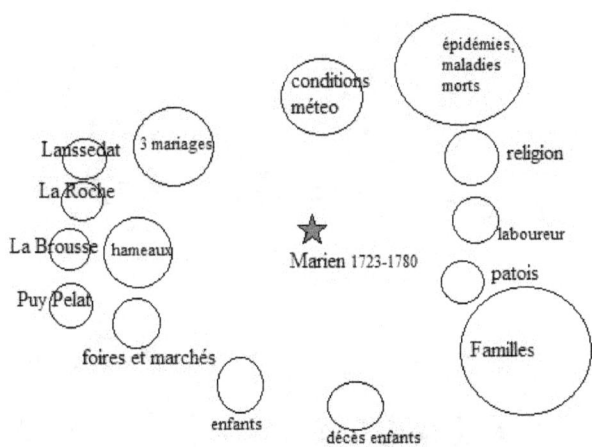

► Mathieu 1834-1898

▶ Louis-Antoine 1894-1940

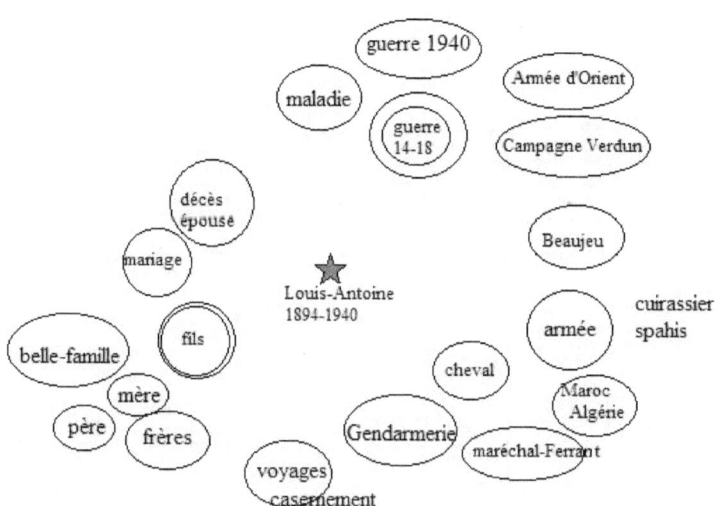

As these three examples show, this type of graph synthetically expresses a person's "environment".

This representation in this form of social atom is particularly rich in teaching and offers a correct summary of a life.

Another form of graph would be to propose for the entire family tree one and only one characterization of an individual: a significant or important fact.

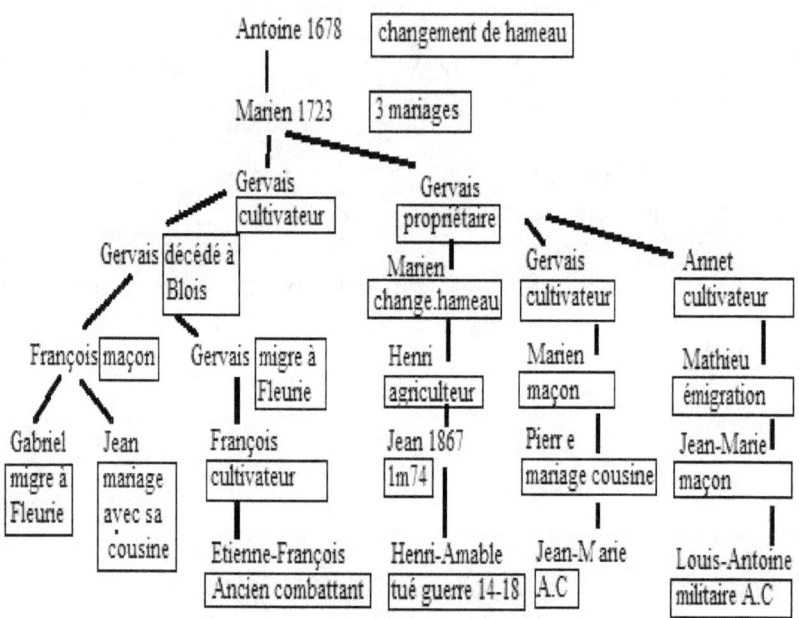

This tree proposes a selection of people and shows characteristic features

Women are under-represented because there is little information available. It is nevertheless interesting to consider their village of origin, the number of children, their profession, their health problems, but also their relationships, their characters, the influence they had on family choices.

There are thus several possible visions of genosociogram. We can thus highlight certain characteristics of a family tree, determine evolutions, point out particular traumas.

The genosociogram is the main tool of psychogenealogy.

This tree records for each of its elements (individuals) the important events in the life of the person and the family, the first names, dates, ages at each of the events, uprooting, occupations, level of education, diseases, wars, etc...

This creates a table that can be used statistically.

The table below has been compiled from known elements that are only figures and are assumed to have been stressful and traumatic.

Each column defines a characteristic that will be called a descriptor. The statistical analysis used is a descriptive analysis that will allow individuals to be grouped according to their similarities in behaviour. The descriptors will not be weighted, i. e. they will not be assigned a coefficient that defines the degree of importance of this characteristic. From a specific point in a tree, there are different family tree "trajectories" determined by continuities or breaks in habits or behaviours. These trajectories, which are more or less disturbed and with more or less variability, can be compared.

The table below defines a number of descriptors. There may be many others, but the further up the tree you go, the more incomplete or inaccurate the information becomes.

We will present several cases of descriptors associated with populations of individuals that differ in number.

Example A :
List of descriptors :

1-Marriage age 0 : no   1: < 20   2: < 30   3: < 40   4: < 50   5: < 60
2-Age of death 1: < 20 2: < 30   3: < 40   4: < 50   5: < 60   6: > 60
3-Age spouse death   1: < 20   2: < 30   3: < 40   4: < 50   5: < 60   6: > 60
4-number of children
5-number of children who died before the age of 5
6-number of children who died between 5 and 10 years of age
7-number of children who died between 10 and 20 years of age

8-TB disease (tuberculose) 0 : no 1 : yes
9-professional change 0 : no 1 : yes
10- violation of the law 0 : no 1 : yes
11-alcoholism 0 : no 1 : yes
12-warring 0: no 1: yes
13-disability 0 : no 1 : yes
14-Deceased to war 0: no 1: yes
15-war injury 0 : no 1 : yes
16 military service 0 : no 1 : yes (completed)
17-changing location 0 : no 1 : yes
18- sex 0 : F 1 : Male

The people studied: A- Beaujolais Branch

a- Mathieu	1833-1898	
b- Jacques	1869-1917	
c- Jean-Marie	1859-1905	
d- Antoine	1886-1919	
e- Jeanne	1887-1910	
f- Jacques	1891-1975	
g- Gaston	1920-1977	
h- Louis-Antoine	1894-1940	
i- Lucien	1924	
j- Jeanne	1835-1899	
k- Jeanne	1896-1933	
l- Valentine	1898-1984	
m- Annet	1793-1862	
n- Antoinette	1801-	
o- Colette	1926	

Table of descriptors :

	1	2	3	4	5	6	7	8	9	10	11	12	13	14	15	16	17	18
a	3	6	6	7	5	0	0	0	0	0	0	0	0	0	0	1	1	1
b	0	3	0	0	0	0	0	0	0	1	0	1	0	0	1	1	0	1
c	2	4	6	8	4	0	0	0	0	0	0	0	0	0	0	1	0	1
d	0	4	0	0	0	0	0	0	1	1	0	1	0	0	1	1	1	1
e	1	1	5	0	0	0	0	0	1	0	0	0	0	0	0	0	1	0
f	2	6	6	1	0	0	0	0	1	0	0	1	1	0	1	0	0	1
g	2	5	2	1	0	0	0	0	1	0	1	0	0	0	0	1	0	1
h	2	4	3	1	0	0	0	1	1	0	0	1	0	1	1	1	1	1
i	2	6	6	3	0	0	0	0	1	0	0	1	0	0	0	1	1	1
j	2	6	6	7	5	0	0	0	0	0	0	0	0	0	0	0	0	0
k	2	3	4	1	0	0	0	0	0	0	0	0	0	0	0	0	1	0
l	2	6	6	1	0	0	0	0	0	0	0	0	0	0	0	0	0	0
m	3	6	6	8	4	0	0	0	0	0	0	0	0	0	0	1	0	1
n	2	4	6	8	4	0	0	0	0	0	0	0	0	0	0	0	0	0
o	2	6	6	3	0	0	0	0	1	0	0	0	0	0	0	0	0	0

The rows represent the people who meet the 18 criteria (columns) This table corresponds to a matrix.

It is possible to synthesize this table with a two-dimensional graph in order to show promiscuity in terms of behaviour between people.

The statistical analysis used in this study is the curvilinear component analysis, the theory of which will be recalled in the appendix pages. the graph has no dimension, it expresses proximity in terms of distance between individuals. The algorithm is a learning method.

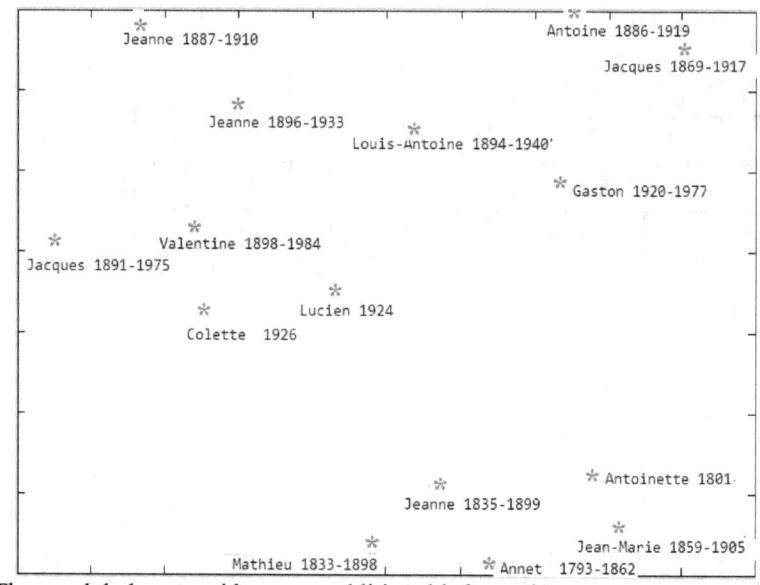

The graph below provides some additional information:

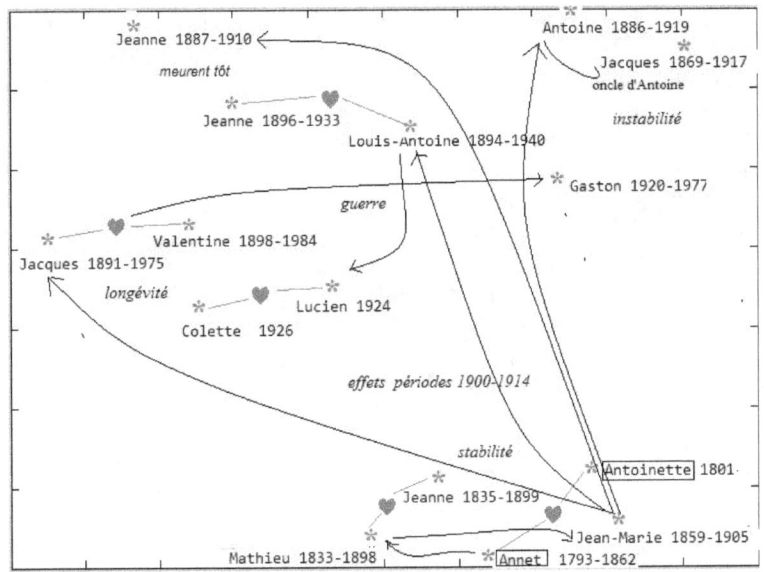

The descriptors are of course very important for the representation. For example, we observe that there have been no remarriages.

In example B below we will modify these descriptors as follows:

1-Marriage age 0 : no   1: < 20   2: < 30   3: < 40   4: < 50   5: < 60
2-Age of death   1: < 20   2: < 30   3: < 40   4: < 50   5: < 60   6: > 60
3-Age spouse death 1: < 20   2: < 30   3: < 40   4: < 50   5: < 60   6: > 60
4-number of children
5-number of children who died before the age of 5
6-position of the studied person in the siblings
7-position of the person if the deceased children are not counted

8-height   0 : <1m7   1 :>1m7
9-professional change   0 : no 1 : yes
10- violation of the law 0 : no 1 : yes
11-Mason or no   0 : no   1 : yes
12-warring   0 : no   1: yes
13-disability   0 : no   1 : yes
14-Deceased to war   0 : no   1 : yes
15-war injury   0 : no   1 : yes
16 military service   0 : no   1 : yes (completed)
17-changing location 0 : no   1 : yes

18- sex   0 : F   1 : Male

The people studied: A- Beaujolais Branch

a- Mathieu	1833-1898
b- Jacques	1869-1917
c- Jean-Marie	1859-1905
d- Antoine	1886-1919
f- Jacques	1891-1975
g- Gaston	1920-1977
h- Louis-Antoine	1894-1940
i- Lucien	1924
m- Annet	1793-1862

The study will focus on the "Male" population

Table of descriptors

	1	2	3	4	5	6	7	8	9	10	11	12	13	14	15	16	17	18
a	3	6	6	7	5	3	2	0	0	0	1	0	0	0	0	1	1	1
b	0	3	0	0	0	5	2	0	0	1	1	1	0	0	1	1	0	1
c	2	4	6	8	4	1	1	0	0	0	1	0	0	0	0	1	0	1
d	0	4	0	0	0	2	1	1	1	1	0	1	0	0	1	1	1	1
f	2	6	6	1	0	4	3	1	1	0	0	1	1	0	1	0	0	1
g	2	5	2	1	0	1	1	1	1	0	0	0	0	0	0	1	0	1
h	2	4	3	1	0	5	4	1	1	0	0	1	0	1	1	1	1	1
i	2	6	6	3	0	1	1	1	1	0	0	1	0	0	0	1	1	1
m	3	6	6	8	4	2	2	0	0	0	1	0	0	0	0	1	0	1

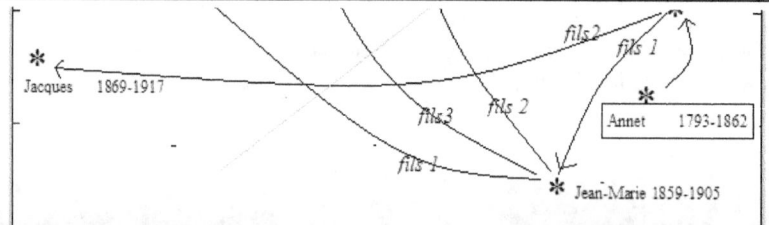

Example C :

The following study will be carried out on the "male" population on the whole tree since Marien 1723-1780 (i.e. the one who had three marriages)

The descriptors will be as follows:

1-Marriage age   0 : no   1: < 20   2: < 30   3: < 40   4: < 50   5: < 60
2-Age of death   1: < 20   2: < 30   3: < 40   4: < 50   5: < 60   6: > 60
3-Age spouse death 1: < 20   2: < 30   3: < 40   4: < 50   5: < 60   6: > 60
4-number of children
5-number of children who died before the age of 5
6-position of the studied person in the siblings
7-position of the person if the deceased children are not counted

8-height   0 : <1m7 1 :>1m7
9-professional change   0 : no 1 : yes
10-change of village   0 : no 1 : yes
11-Mason or no   0 : no 1 : yes
12-farmer or not   0 : no 1 : yes
13-warring   0: no 1: yes
14-Deceased to war   0: no 1: yes
15-war injury   0: no 1 : yes
16 military service   0: no 1 : yes (completed)
17-changing location (region) 0: no 1 : yes
18- several marriages   0: no 1 : yes

The people studied:

1- Mathieu   1833-1898
2- Jacques   1869-1917
3- Jean-Marie   1859-1905
4- Antoine   1886-1919
5- Jacques   1891-1975
6- Gaston   1920-1977
7- Louis-Antoine   1894-1940
8- Lucien   1924
9- Annet   1793-1862
10-Marien   1723-1780
11- Marien   1723-1780
12- Marien   1723-1780
13- Gervais   1751
14- Gervais   1788-
15- Gervais   1819-1886
16- Gervais   1819-1886
17- François   1851-
18- Jean   1859-1904
19- François   1817-1881
20- Gabriel   1854-
21- Gabriel   1854-
22 - Félix-Gervais   1889-1929
23- Marien   1792-1868
24- Jean   1867-1913
25- Henri-Amable   1893-1918
26- Marien   1815-1862
27- Gervais   1846-1883
28- André   1873-1908
29- Jean   1874-1910
30- Pierre   1851-1900
31- Jacques   1864 -1900
32- Henri   1836

	1	2	3	4	5	6	7	8	9	10	11	12	13	14	15	16	17	18
1	3	6	6	7	5	3	2	0	0	0	1	0	0	0	0	1	1	0
2	0	3	0	0	0	5	2	0	0	0	1	1	0	0	1	1	0	0
3	2	4	6	8	4	1	1	0	0	0	1	0	0	0	0	1	0	0
4	0	4	0	0	0	2	1	1	1	1	0	1	0	0	1	1	1	0
5	2	6	6	1	0	4	3	1	1	0	0	1	1	0	1	0	0	0
6	2	5	2	1	0	1	1	1	1	0	0	0	0	0	0	1	0	0
7	2	4	3	1	0	5	4	1	1	1	0	1	0	1	1	1	1	0
8	2	6	6	3	0	1	1	1	1	1	0	1	0	0	0	1	1	0
9	3	6	6	8	4	2	2	0	0	0	1	0	0	0	0	1	0	0
10	1	5	3	3	1	3	2	0	0	0	0	1	0	0	0	0	0	1
11	1	5	3	2	2	3	2	0	0	0	0	1	0	0	0	0	0	1
12	1	5	3	1	0	3	2	0	0	0	0	1	0	0	0	0	0	1
13	3	3	3	2	1	3	3	0	0	1	0	1	0	0	0	0	0	0
14	2	3	6	4	1	2	2	0	1	1	1	0	0	0	0	0	0	0
15	2	5	2	0	0	3	3	0	1	1	1	0	0	0	0	0	1	1
16	3	5	5	4	1	3	3	0	1	1	1	0	0	0	0	0	1	1
17	3	6	6	4	1	1	1	0	0	0	0	1	0	0	0	0	0	0
18	2	3	4	1	1	4	4	0	1	1	1	0	0	0	0	0	1	0
19	3	6	6	5	2	2	2	0	0	0	1	0	0	0	0	0	0	0
20	3	4	5	2	1	1	1	0	0	1	1	0	0	0	0	0	1	1

21	4	4	4	1	0	1	1	0	0	1	1	0	0	0	0	0	1	1
22	2	3	4	2	0	2	2	1	0	0	0	1	1	0	1	1	0	0
23	3	4	6	11	7	2	2	0	0	1	0	1	0	0	0	0	0	0
24	2	4	5	1	0	3	3	1	0	0	1	0	0	0	0	0	0	0
25	0	2	0	0	0	1	1	1	0	1	1	1	1	1	1	1	1	0
26	3	4	4	2	0	1	1	0	0	0	1	0	0	0	0	1	0	0

27	2	3	3	2	0	1	1	1	0	0	1	0	0	0	0	1	0	0
28	1	3	4	0	0	1	1	1	0	0	1	0	1	1	0	1	1	0
29	2	3	5	4	0	2	2	1	0	0	0	1	0	0	0	1	0	0
30	2	4	4	2	0	2	2	1	0	0	1	0	0	0	0	0	0	0
31	2	4	5	1	1	1	1	1	0	0	1	0	0	0	0	0	0	0
32	2	3	4	3	0	7	3	1	0	0	0	1	0	0	0	0	0	0

The graph by the CCA algorithm giving a view of the similarities in behaviour of the different men studied gives the following representation:

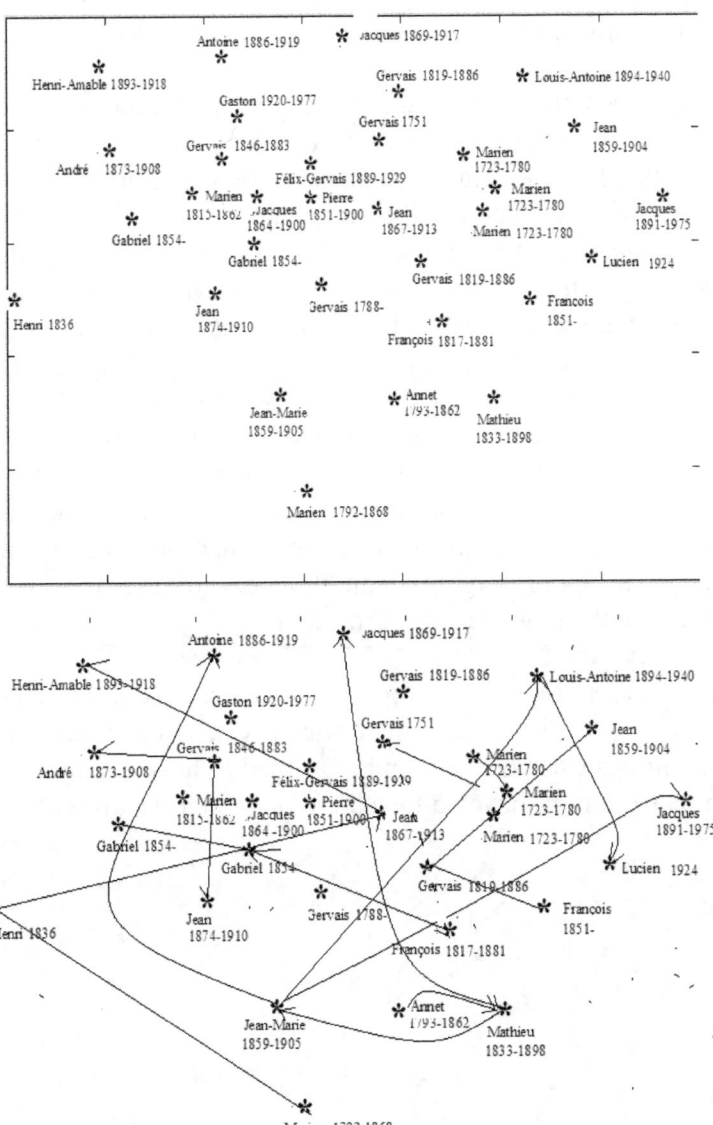

What to remember:

The representation is linked to the types and number of descriptors: thus, in the whole tree, several cases of changes can be observed: the period of the First World War plays a very important role in the observed changes, then comes the period described as the second part of the 19th century when temporary and then permanent emigrations are observed. We will also remember the importance of the change of profession; in these examples, the professions, at least until the 19th century, can be summarized as that of farmer (owner or operator) and mason.

The deaths of one (or both) members of the couple, remarriages, deaths of children have created traumas but without altering people's life "trajectory". The economic difficulties associated with famines, themselves linked to the difficult weather conditions at the time and associated with poor hygiene conditions according to our current definitions, are the main causes of mortality.

This representation mode allows you to visualize the differences in path between branches of a tree. A branch whose members are spread over the entire surface of the map is assumed to have encountered more different cases and to have followed a more chaotic path without being negative.

Chapter 6

Psychogenealogy and Social Psychology

The in-depth analysis of the family tree showed how important the role of the hamlet (or village) is as a social structure. A hamlet is a group of dwellings belonging to different families or cousins.

A hamlet or village thus forms a group. But we observe that there are other groups in which a person lives.

The following graph summarizes these groups as a social atom.

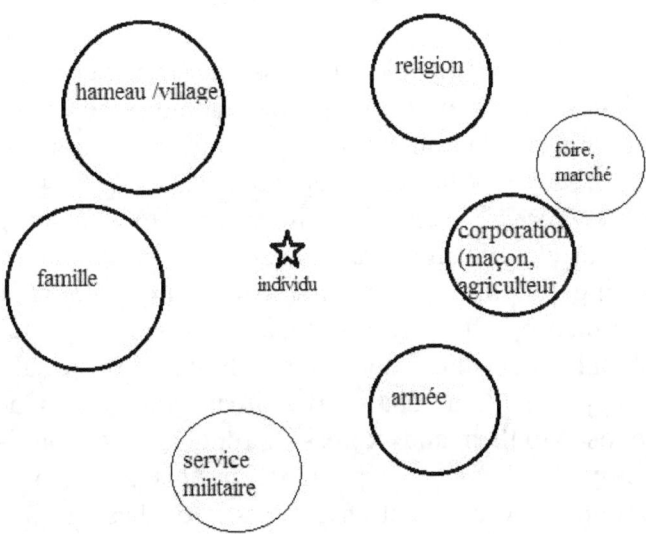

The examination of these operations will make it possible to understand the modes of integration and functioning as well as the conditions in which these people have expressed themselves.

The hamlet was therefore the first social authority that enclosed these people in concrete situations and linked them to other people with whom they interacted for several generations.

We found that since men married late and died early, children knew little about their fathers. This is all the more true if the father was a bricklayer and therefore absent for many months or weeks. The "hamlet" group therefore interacted very strongly with the "family" group, even if it is understood in its broadest sense (with uncles, aunts, cousins).

A group is an organized social whole with specific components and through the forms of relationships and communications it generates. Thus a hamlet or village develops relational processes and produces specific forms of influence, thus determining positions between members of the group.

One might think that masons, because of their regular migrations could free themselves from these links. In reality, this is not the case. The masons travelled together, if possible from the same village or nearby villages, they went to work in the same place (here Beaujolais, Beaujeu and Fleurie, but others went to Lyon). They were housed in the same house, always speaking the same dialect. Remaining in this group, they were subject to very little influence from other groups and protected themselves from interactions.

Belonging to this group has been an essential element in maintaining their psychological balance.

The hamlet or village and even religion form what is called a primary group[66], i.e. individuals have direct relationships, adhere to the values proposed to them and express a strong sense of cohesion.

A family, a group of neighbours, friends are also examples of primary groups. The essential characteristic of these groups is that the relationships between members are immediate and personal.

Society is a secondary group because relationships are more code-determined and members have more or less imposed relationships between them during the time they are together.

---

66 Colley 1909

The army can be considered as a secondary group especially in its "military service" phase. For a person who will join the army, it can become a primary group.

A second distinction concerns the distinction between formal and informal groups. Within a village, each member had for several generations an assigned place and a prescribed role, more or less implicitly imposing a certain hierarchy. Nevertheless, many informal groups have been formed through encounters, travel, for example, or simply through pre-marriage relationships with other families in other villages. In any case, everyone was identified by the place and social status they occupied and through the role they occupied.

A third distinction concerns home groups and reference groups[67]. The groups to which we belong and which are supposed to have a significant influence on our attitudes and values only partially fulfil this role[68]. Not all members of this family tree have adopted the behavioural norms of their groups. They were able to take as reference the norms of their wife's group, for example, or of the village where they went to live. These changes could have been made by comparing these standards with each other, by evaluating them, or simply by adopting them. In the latter situation, we should note the emotional characteristics, enthusiasm, passivity, or rejection with its form of violence.

In Auvergne, the root of the family tree, everyone had a place in the group, where types of familiar interactions were played out; everyone was therefore integrated into various social groups. The group (village) could therefore be identified by durable elements that identified and structured it.

A village imposes a model of conduct on each inhabitant, linked to the group's expectations. But this role is not fixed and evolves over time. There may be conflicts because the input of external ideas can

---

67 Hyman 1942
68 G-N FisherG-N Fisher

change the group's behaviour, but the balance is achieved either by integrating these ideas or by the departure of the person carrying these ideas. The permanent departures of some may be explained by this scenario.

Mathieu left around 1850 for Beaujeu. He therefore resigned himself to adopting other group standards. Knowing that his wife was fatherless, this family unit was therefore very small. By having seven children, he may have wanted (unwillingly or unconsciously) to recreate a group in an attempt to preserve the identity of his home group. The high mortality has prevented this realization. His first son Jean-Marie also had eight children, was it in the same spirit? The high mortality also prevented the creation of a group. The remaining children then dispersed geographically, cutting themselves off from their original roots. The stories of some of them show that this loss of group standards has resulted in a loss of control over their environment.

Does the departure for the army of Jean-Marie's sons correspond to the desire to find a new psychological field allowing them to express themselves or to modify the spirit of the family group?

To analyze a family tree is also to be interested in group phenomena, because a family, a village, a corporation form groups influencing certain aspects of collective life.

The army and the Church are two types of interesting organizations to study within which it is possible to approach the relationships between the psychological functioning of the individual and the collective situation. The case of the army is of particular interest to us since Jean-Marie and his brothers Jacques and Antoine (but also other cousins) stayed there for several years.

According to Freud, the functioning of the army (and the Church) is based on the existence of a leader who loves all members equally and on the emotional bonds between the members themselves; but as Freud pointed out, the leader's love for members is in fact only an illusion; the bonds between the leader and the members of an organization are based on unconscious processes of which identification is one of the main forms of expression.

For Freud, the leader is a model; he is therefore the object of an archaic attachment on the part of the members because he represents their ideal of the Self ("Moi").

This link also exists between the members themselves; they discover common traits that allow them to consider themselves as equal among themselves; in this way, identification makes it possible to constitute a factor of social cohesion.

It is therefore surprising that some members of the family tree studied went into the army after being separated from their group of origin, the numerous disappearances of relatives, their situation as orphans in search of a father, and difficulties in professional integration.

This quest for links seems to have resulted in an acceptance of the relationships offered by the army. It should also be noted that at that time the army had restored its image among the people and offered employment, training, but also a rich, varied and regular diet.

The army offered them their need for protection with the side effect of putting them in a position of dependence.

A group is formed in relation to situations of dependence; thus it exists only in function and in relation to the central person around whom it is organized; in the case of a family it is the patriarch, in a more informal organization it is the leader (or the tyrant); a group can also exist around a hero (frequent in the army), a person of bad influence (we find this case in the family tree) or good example (this case is less visible perhaps because it is more general). These figures, objects of repulsion or identification, will nevertheless play an important role in the construction of their personality by producing a certain number of emotional reactions revealing their affective structure and those of the generation or generations that will follow. We can see here the importance of joining groups, especially since they allow them to respond in part to their anguish about the outside world and its reality.

Thus, leaving his village, a member of a family community had to assess the situation by moving to another place; it could have been favourable or unfavourable depending on the possibilities for living that this new place offers him

Then he moved on to a phase of socialization, adapting to a new group, getting married and thus joining other families, which had more or less different rules of life or behaviour.

The adaptation phase is generally a success thanks to the births but also to the deaths that will test and create a cohesion of the group. The mason's job leads men to leave. This situation is not insignificant because each time he returns he will have to re-socialize herself, redefine her role within this community but also within her couple because being very often absent, the wife has taken a lot of autonomy and responsibility. There comes a time when this resocialization process no longer succeeds so well that this person is forced to leave the group. This situation may be one of the explanations for the permanent departures.

Women have been leaving for centuries to marry far from their villages of origin, integrating other families and groups. It is easy to imagine the importance of the traumas they have experienced and which are never mentioned.

When leaving Auvergne's region, the men did not find any elements that would facilitate a certain new cohesion[69]; success could have been a factor of cohesion, but obviously it was not there. The premature deaths of parents and children have hindered this development. This situation still has a positive effect to the extent that, since cohesion was weak, group members had few ties and little tendency to conform to standards. The impact of a group's compliance was therefore reduced, they gained in freedom of action.

---

69 Festinger (1952) : la cohésion est la somme de toutes les forces agissant sur les membres d'un groupe afin de les y maintenir

Thus, in the absence of an autocratic model expressed through centralized decision-making, due to the absence of the father, the model adopted by the three brothers, Jean-Marie, Antoine and Jacques, was rather consultative, being summarized by exchanges, which perhaps explains why the brothers joined the army with the exception of the eldest who, as a family head, had difficulty assuming this role for which he was not intended.

Did the older brother have an influence on his brothers and sister? And in general, does a child's hierarchical position within a sibling influence his or her leadership and the way in which he or she guides group members? These questions are difficult to answer in the affirmative when looking at the entire family tree.

The study of signatures could have provided us with some valuable information about the writing, the size of the signature, its position, its hesitant or assertive style. In the lack of this information, the physical and psychological characteristics of these people are not available to define their leadership status. If we consider that tall size, self-esteem, need for accomplishment, self-confidence are necessary to be a leader, then we can say that this feeling is mixed concerning the people studied, they are rather independent people.

The disease has been a major factor in trauma. It is not enough to simply record its effects from a statistical point of view by counting deaths. The psychological effects are undeniable and poorly measured or taken into account, as are the psychosocial factors involved in the development and progression of certain diseases.

For a long time it was suspected that psychological factors played a role in the disease and its onset[70]. But this dimension was relegated to the secondary elements.

The study of these factors consists in identifying the elements that are likely to cause the disease, such as the cultural context, social category, lifestyle, more personal characteristics or environmental factors.

---

70 Exemple Descarte R « Lettres, œuvres et lettres », Paris, Gallimard

In he many studies of the causes that may play a role in the development and progression of diseases, it is the stress factor[71] associated with events that cause a significant life change that appears to be one of the most essential. It has been shown that at the psychological level, stress is manifested by an activation of the hormonal system, i. e. by a physiological reaction that manifests itself in three phases.

The first phase is an alarm reaction that mobilizes the body to stimulate its defence.

The second phase is an adaptation phase where the body attempts to recover its lost energy and repair the lost damage.

The third phase is an exhaustion phase which is characterized by a decrease in resistance in the event that the body cannot control and manage stress.

But if these phases are a bit mechanical visions of the processes, they nevertheless remain quite meaningful. In addition, they must be given the ability to react to these events, i.e. to take into account cognitive and emotional factors.

Stress can be considered[72] as a process in which the individual assesses the situation he or she is facing according to the resources at his or her disposal, which he or she believes do not allow him or her to cope.

This conceptualization of stress made it possible to establish a scale of stressful events, even if not all individuals had the same reaction to the same stressful events.

It has been shown that those who had experienced stressful events in the past ten years had contracted in a large majority of cases significant health problems.

Studies have also shown that the loss of a vital link is one of the most important events in life. Studies have shown that death rates are always higher at all ages among those who have lost their spouses.

---

71 Le concept de stress a été introduit par Selye (1956)
72 Travaux de Lazarus et Folkman (1984)

If we look at the entire family tree, we see that it is characterized by the premature deaths of men (remember that men married late, were often absent, and were more in contact with outbreaks of various diseases).

The women were widows at a relatively young age, and others died in childbirth.

Infant mortality was very high.

Hygiene conditions were very unhealthy.

The diet was deficient and unbalanced

Weather conditions were extreme in the 17th, 18th and 19th centuries.

Some stress events were less important at those times than if they were experienced now, because they were part of everyday life or ancestral habits. Nevertheless, a death and its consequences on the lifestyle of the survivors had significant consequences on the life "trajectory" of the descendants.

When Jean-Marie died at 45 in 1905, his wife Benoite probably had great financial difficulties raising her children, considering the jobs she had done and the places she lived in. This woman had to show great strength of character because the same year she lost her husband in May, she married her daughter in June (she died 5 years later), and lost her last son in October (he was 5 years old). It is necessary to take into account the events that occurred to his daughter in 1907 and more generally during the period 1905-1910. These events must have caused great disruption to all members of this family.

Jean-Marie's father, Mathieu, saw 4 of his 6 children die.

His wife died a year after his death.

Louis-Antoine, Jean-Marie's son, saw his wife die at the age of 37 of an illness after less than ten years of marriage, only finding herself alone to raise her son, who himself was orphaned by both parents six years later.

As already mentioned, throughout this family tree, children were orphaned very early on and were raised by elders, family circles or the village community.

As stress factors, we must rely on migration to another region, changes in occupation, the transition from rural to urban life, the transition from agriculture to manufacturing, that is, from living outdoors to living in a confined, unhealthy environment at that time, to major changes in the rhythms of life.

The effects of the First World War have been the subject of numerous studies on the traumas suffered by those who returned, but also by spouses, children and community life disrupted by all these changes.

Another stress factor is the transition from patois to French as a language of communication and the increase in the level of education since the end of the 19th century thanks to the laws on compulsory education.

The end of the 19th century and the beginning of the 20th century were therefore a period of high tension with significant and probably unsuspected psychological effects.

In addition to the factors mentioned above, another factor involved in the onset or development of a disease or physical impairment is the person's personality. It seems that there is a link between stress and cardiovascular disorders, even if we know nothing about the diseases they may have had about the family tree studied. However, it should be noted that the personality traits we encounter in our time are very different from those encountered at least a century ago; feelings of competitiveness, the notion of urgency, forms of aggressiveness and hostility are probably different. However, it has been shown that the anxiety associated with hostility is an important factor in the onset of disease.

The people in the family tree studied had good reason to be anxious about their future in the face of an unfavourable present. It does not seem that any hostility, for example, towards institutions or their immediate environment, could be noted. This feature does not mean that they have been inhibited in the expression of their emotions, or that they have adopted attitudes of submission or altruistic attitudes that are also factors in the development of diseases, especially cancers. Perhaps they had cancers that were not predicted under this name at the time.

Studies[73] have shown that those who have a fighting spirit in the face of illness have a longer life expectancy than those who have attitudes of acceptance or denial. The society in which these people lived favoured acceptance and submission, which could explain, to a small extent, these early deaths.

Only a small part because ancestral beliefs about these events, which were repeated from generation to generation, had an effect on their ability to adapt to these familiar situations. In any case, these people did not have excessive optimism about a future that persisted in remaining gloomy.

What beliefs might have increased a person's emotional reaction to a stressful event that could have weakened their ability to adapt? Probably the energy diffused by the group formed by a family circle and the village is an important factor. The exit of these groups has weakened some people: the study of the family tree shows that people from the branch that remained in the village of origin (La Roche) were less vulnerable than those who were in other villages or even worse in other regions.

Jeanne, Louis-Antoine's wife, died at the age of 37 following a medical operation at the Villefranche sur Saône hospital. Louis-Antoine died six years later at the age of 46, also of an illness. He joined the army at the age of 18, then campaigned in Morocco and Algeria (1st and 5th Spahis Regiments), he campaigned in Verdun before leaving for the Eastern army. On his return he joined the Gendarmerie and married in 1922. His marriage lasted less than 10 years. This simple reminder shows the succession of traumas he had to endure, gradually weakening him.

For several years he was confronted with death. This one concerned him directly and personally. Two years of hospitalization and treatment during which he remained lucid about the fatal outlet, enrolling his 16-year-old son in the Lorient Naval Academy before his death. This helplessness in the face of the disease has resulted in positive action for the future.

---

73 Pettingale et coll. 1985

This family has overcome many hardships, which can be considered as reinforcing hardships that would give the impression of overcoming headwinds with a strong sense of personal effectiveness. But this whole family has actually been psychologically weakened for a long time. In the face of invasive information about the ever-present death, the filters erected as a defence system have largely cracked, reinforcing the vulnerability factor.

The environments in which we live and work have a strong influence on our behaviour. From a psychological point of view, the environment is understood on several levels. For the members of this family, most of whom were Masons, the social framework was extended to the region. For Louis-Antoine, this framework was much broader, because the physical places were extended, for the first time in this family, to countries such as Morocco, Algeria, the countries of Eastern Europe, then Northern France. This space was also restricted to a group formed by the army or the Gendarmerie. It was actually this space that was occupied by Louis-Antoine. Her wedding added a different extra space. The processes of human-environment interaction are in fact quite complex with systems of codes and social norms that coexist. All these environments have therefore constituted Louis-Antoine's human territory and shaped his way of life.

We all establish a personal sphere, where we arrange our interactions between ourselves and others. This space is variable for everyone because the distances established between us and others are different.

It is a protective space, a buffer zone, composed of several successive layers that are opened or closed according to the occasion. Thus personal space is expressed in our relationships with others through the establishment of certain distances according to the situation in which we find ourselves.

The way people in the family tree studied used these distances has changed significantly over time.

Personal spaces were very different when people lived more or less in communities in villages and hamlets. These spaces opened up, layers were added when some left as masons to other terroirs. The final migrations have redistributed these personal spaces, strengthening them but more likely weakening them. This process has become dynamic, weakening people. The notions of distance, public, social, personal, intimate, have evolved, thus changing behaviours and lifestyles and ways of thinking.

The importance given to personal space is not a universal fact; it depends on the cultural characteristics that will make personal space a factor of expression of the value and place of the individual. Thus in the army, inter-personal exchanges are associated with great physical proximity, so personal space will be reduced. On the other hand, inter-personal exchanges between two groups, the army and the civil space, will be greater, leading to a larger personal space.

A territory, in environmental psychology, applied to the human and social context, refers to the developed spaces that constitute social frameworks and reveal socio-cultural characteristics. A territory is therefore a socially occupied space. The uses of this space have therefore changed considerably over time, leading to major social changes.

The primary territory, like the farm where there was only one room where the whole family lived, has been divided into several private spaces with bedrooms, bathrooms... The secondary territory, designated as the village, used by one or more cohabiting groups, has evolved because it has expanded, and the codes and rituals have evolved more or less strongly in the same way as the social norms of the group and the duration of occupation of this space.

The public territory has grown and changed considerably, with increasingly less temporary space occupancy times requiring the implementation of tacit, informal and regulated rules of use.

Analysing a family tree also means analysing all forms of change, such as those in spaces, in order to better understand the cultural and social evolution of its members. For example, the type of house, furniture, taste, preferences, aesthetic arrangement of things, can provide a lot of information about people's characters; a space can be sociopaedic, i.e. arranged in such a way as to facilitate exchanges, or the opposite, if the arrangement rather causes separation and isolation between people.

During this succession of generations, people's mental image of their environment evolved until it was completely altered at the end of the 19th century and the beginning of the 20th century.

This organized representation of the environment in which they interacted has evolved so much that it has only resulted in a number of traumas or stresses because this representation provides not the environment as it is, but as they believe it is. The gap can be very large. The image we have of an environment will affect the way we behave in that environment.

This representation is in fact the result of a process, a learning process that provides the person with information in order to locate and orient themselves in their space.

Geographical movements, migrations, disruptions within the family environment, social changes and a fortiori a war and its consequences, are vectors of this loss of reference. Very often the cognitive map is deficient because the information received has been poorly selected, decoded and reorganized. The mental image that people had of a field, of the countryside is different from the image they had of a factory, i.e. a closed space, or the mental image of a village in relation to the image of a city.

This transition from the countryside to the city reveals an important criterion, that of the effects of densification. Density has led to a number of social problems, which, according to some research, have only intensified the expression of pre-existing behaviours or emotions initiated by other motives.

The partitioning of farmers in factories has accentuated this phenomenon, which is linked to the feeling of loss of freedom, leading to a change in behaviour. As for the masons, they have practiced in a larger living space without it being satisfactory given the long absences, a source of stress for some according to the levels of adaptation of each.

These losses of reference points, the delay in adaptation, the lack of appropriation and personalization of their new living space were disruptive elements that generated strong stress situations.

In the Combrailles region, people gradually appropriated the space without too much difficulty as they settled in villages or hamlets close to each other. Thus the relationships between people were not lost, at most distended, but the cousins remained in contact for several centuries. The people (or group) who leave always try to recreate the framework of the initial space. It is gradually that it is changing. For those who left for urban areas, they were subjected to the phenomenon of isolation, the feeling of crowding, noise, and changes in social relations.

For decades, life has been organized around work. It has always been an important aspect in everyone's experience and in everyone's contribution to the life of a group (family, village). The men in the family tree have always had a job, a specialization driven by the know-how of the previous generation. This work, out of necessity, made it possible to create and maintain links between the members of the group (village).

At the beginning of the century, the upheavals in society, ideological trends and new technologies generated many psychological disorders whose effects are still felt over several generations, including a redefinition of labour value and the emergence of unemployment and the notion of retirement.

Another group has emerged, the company (entreprise), which is not only an economic entity, but also an organized social group with its own values. We will have to interact differently with others, learn other rules of the game. Other behaviours will have to be adopted according to prescribed roles, linked to its tasks and function. It may or may not adhere to the request of society: the framework of this socialization is a complex process and is limited to the particular context in which the person evolves.

These mutations have had an impact on the lives of the members of this tree as well as on all family trees. Integration for many has not been a simple formality, some of them having experienced the profound trauma of the unemployment experience, practically leading to a high vulnerability from which deep psychological symptoms follow.

Chapter 7

Cognitive models in psychogenealogy
A few words...

A family tree is a graphical representation of a person's ascending or descending family tree. It is a structured representation of the family ties between individuals that are most often represented in the form of a tree with its roots, trunk, branches, leaves, the tree grows stronger as the ascendants are discovered. In descending genealogy, research is carried out on a given individual and aims to find all his descendants. In general, we consider that we read from top to bottom and from the oldest to the youngest. But there are other representations such as a circular or semi-circular representation.

However, these trees remain representations on a plane, i.e. in two dimensions. If this reading is easy and remains satisfactory, we nevertheless miss a certain amount of information that is not possible to visualize in this context.

Thus, we could prefer a three-dimensional representation where the notion of time and thus the "temporal distance" between people would appear, just as we could make the proximity of people and events appear and introduce the genosociogram into the family tree.
We will present below some examples of representations

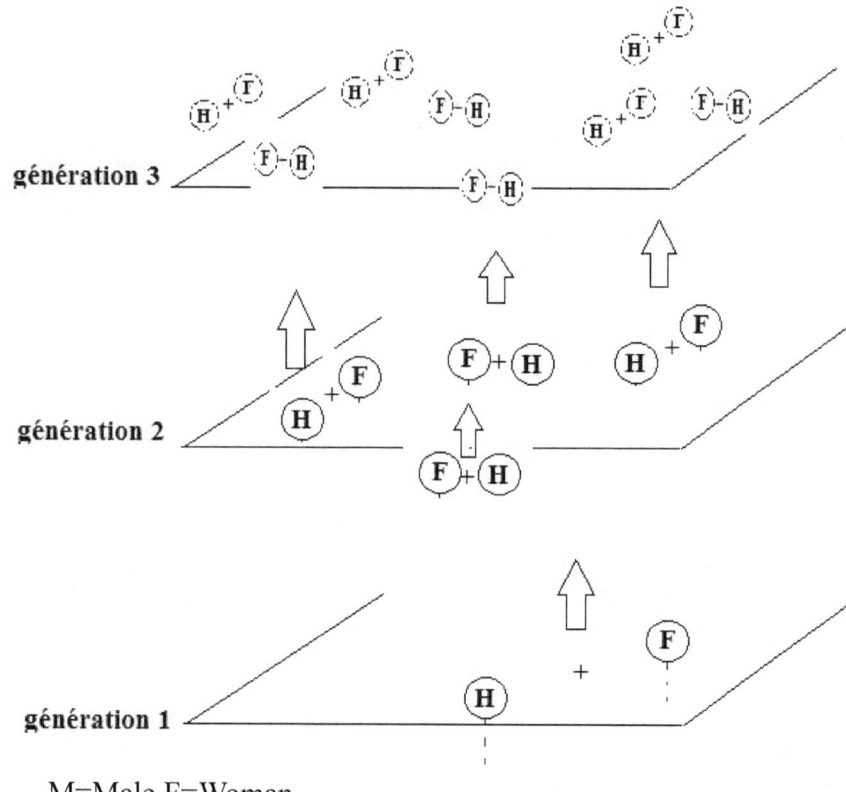

génération 3

génération 2

génération 1

M=Male F=Woman

This representation reveals the notion of time: each member of a generation is distant from the previous and next generation, i.e. the last of a sibling is close in time to the first child that the eldest child of the sibling had. On these graphs we can position the cousins and visualize their degree of distance. This type of representation can be achieved by considering only the dates of birth, dates of death, duration of marriages, or a mixed representation of the whole. This brings us back to what has already been pointed out in this document on the real relationships between the members of a family tree.

On this figure, the genosociogram of each individual can be juxtaposed. Social atoms can be the same or different for different individuals. If they are identical, they may have a different "weight", more or less strong, a significant power of attraction or not, an aspect limited in time.

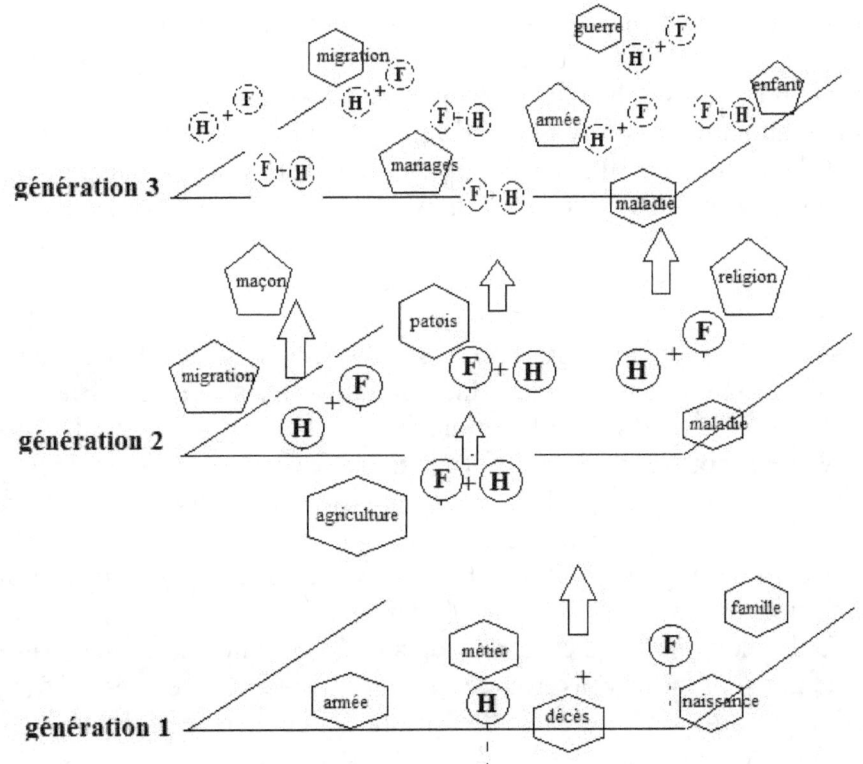

This form of representation is complex to set up even if the resulting information is very interesting. For this reason, this question will be approached from a more scientific perspective in the form of cognitive models.

We have seen that at our birth we are carriers of a quantity of information through our Unconscious Mind.

Then we gradually build ourselves through the interaction of our social atoms but also of the social atoms of the previous generation and the one that follows us. There are no precise limits between generations and each atom evolves in size, importance and attractiveness.

We actually know little about our ancestors. If we have photos, we have their physical characteristics, if we have letters or signatures we understand some of their personality traits. But that's about it.

We know nothing about their emotions, their behaviours, their motivations, their objectives, their desires, their needs. We know nothing about their ability to perceive the world and events, nothing yet about their strategies for developing and organizing knowledge. Social structures were different from now, our ancestors were also less cultivated and their openness to the world was much less; despite this, we can wonder if the cognitive mechanisms were significantly different from ours.

How did they manage conflicts, how did they develop a meta-knowledge based on managing their failures and successes? Has this knowledge benefited future generations?

We do not know if any of them have had any psychological problems at any time in their lives and what the consequences have been on their immediate environment.

We will always know little about our ancestors, we will never hear their voices and we will never meet their eyes.

Did they have the same unconscious impulses, the same conceptions of beauty as we do, even if some choices result from routines engraved little by little in the circuits of the brain over thousands of generations.

The ethological approach[74] teaches us that the first learning took place by reproducing, copying the gestures, attitudes and behaviours of an adult that the learner takes as a model. Hence the importance of the family duplicating its rules and codes.

---

74 L'éthologie se définit originellement comme l'étude des comportements instinctifs puis, actuellement, plus généralement, comme la biologie du comportement
Ethology is originally defined as the study of instinctive behaviour and, currently, more generally, as the biology of behaviour

In default, the child will copy the group or groups to which he or she is closest. Thereafter he will seek to concretize what he has learned and internalized. It should be noted, however, that the mechanisms of acquisition are different from one individual to another, that some are more receptive to concrete aspects, that others have great difficulty in abstracting, in thinking only about concepts. Can we say that there are predispositions? Let us be careful because the formation of cognitive mechanisms is complex.

Thought itself was only mentioned very late, a few decades ago, because thought has no weight, no form, it is ephemeral and elusive, very difficult to conceptualize, thought has not been a tangible reality until now. What could be the way of thinking of our ancestors? Probably very different from ours. For millennia the world had thus a reduced dimension leading us to consider history only from facts.

The role of the group to which the person belongs is important. Thus the people of the branch that left Auvergne encountered many difficulties, probably because the new groups they joined were not strong enough; these groups are mainly the new families from marriages. How have the exchanges between the different members been structured, in quality and quantity? Mathieu (1834-1898) married Jeanne D and entered a very small family, his wife was fatherless at the time of the marriage. Most of her children did not survive, which prevented the formation of a family group. His eldest son Jean-Marie, when he married Benoite B, joined a family with quite strong ties between its members. As Benoite has only sisters, Jean-Marie may have had difficulty expressing his feelings.

Les atomes sociaux mettent en évidence l'importance de la notion de groupe soulevant les questions suivantes :

Was the family group structured, and did it see itself as a group, a sum of individuals?

–   Was there a leader, or several leaders in these family groups, and were they in competition? This implies a risk of group fracture, or a risk of domination. Perhaps that was the case.

–   How were the exchanges within the group conducted in terms of quality, quantity and variety?

–   Did the members of these groups behave rather positively or negatively? What was the distribution of skills and motivation of its members?

How has the group positioned itself in terms of autonomy within the community?

–   Did the members of these groups have a sense of class, in other words, did they realize that there were people who were much better educated and much richer than they were?

–   These questions are important and may explain some of the difficulties faced by family members. The army was an issue for some of these members, it was a matter of opportunity, just as others at the same time joined the unions en masse at the beginning of the century. The emergence and strength of trade unions are concomitant with the fact that people from the countryside migrated to the cities to work hard in factories. As a result, they had lost all membership in their home groups, so the unions, like the army, offered them the opportunity to join a group with people who had new and strong ties.

A few parts of theory....

Social-cognitive theory considers 3 variables:
behavioural factors
environmental factors (extrinsic)
personal (intrinsic) factors
These 3 variables in social cognitive theory are said to be related to each other, causing learning to occur. An individual's personal experience may converge with behavioural and environmental determinants.
In person-environment interaction, human beliefs, ideas and cognitive skills are modified by external factors such as father or mother, family, a stressful environment or a climatic anomaly for example.

In person-behaviour interaction, a person's cognitive processes affect their behaviour, in the same way, the performance of such behaviour can change their way of thinking.

Finally, the interaction between environment and behaviour, external factors can change the way behaviour is displayed. In addition, our behaviour can affect and modify our environment.

These few sentences mean above all that we evolve in a favourable way with maximum efficiency if we remain in a favourable environment.

We can see the difficulty that all the members of this family tree had in simply acquiring elements that facilitate the learning of vital processes.

For generations this learning has been observational learning, most often by acquiring the knowledge of other close people and then reproducing the acquired behaviours. Some have sought to improve their knowledge, without knowing what motivated them and how they achieved their goals. How did they cope with stressful environments and how did they control themselves? Alcohol at that time was one of the solutions to these issues. This information is of course missing, but it can be written in a filigram if you are very cautious.

The attention we attach to things or certain events may, of course, depend on their very characteristics.

But more often than not, it responds to a "need to do something": motivation. This need may be related to survival; we then select the information that can lead to the alleviation of hunger, thirst or even the avoidance of a danger. This motivation has been strongly present for generations.

Sometimes it is a matter of occupying time and our attention is then focused on the environmental stimuli most likely to respond to this motivation. However, most of the time, we orient our behaviour according to the perceptions that will make us carry out an ongoing project or plan for the more or less long term.

This notion of motivation is interesting in that we already perceive that its meaning is different according to the generations and the social status of the person: the motivation of a person with little education and poverty is different from that of an educated and well-off person. The world is perceived differently or must we say that there are several worlds, some of which have remained inaccessible for many unless their cognitive processes are adapted?

Chapter 8

The accents

A family tree is not only a succession of names, it also has great markers of time, such as accent and language.

For each generation we observe that people speak different languages with local patois that evolve over time according to the close communication links with neighbouring regions.

Auvergne emigrants (but also emigrants from other regions in general) who went to Paris, the North, Alsace, Brittany and Provence did not always understand in the 19th century the inhabitants of the regions where they went to work. It is also, among other reasons, why they stayed with each other. Even within a common region, people differentiated themselves by their accent even if they used the same dialect. These differences were geographical but also generational; it is not certain that we understand our 1900s ancestor, and these last ones their 1800s ancestors.

The accents are as old as the language. In the 16th century, French, which had developed during the demographic boom of the Paris basin in the 12th and 13th centuries, was still not very widespread in France. We spoke various languages, different dialects from the languages of "oc" or "oïl", or from non roman varieties such as Basque, Breton and Flemish or Alsatian dialects. Today, these minority languages are in danger of disappearing, but the accents are still resistant in many regions.

An accent is perceived only to the extent that it deviates from a language that is the norm and this has been imposed by the capital's elites and elders[75]. We have to go back to the 17th century, it's not so old. At that time the king's entourage refocused around Paris, then Versailles. In 1647, one of the first French academicians, Vaugelas, defined the correct use of the language as "the way of speaking about the healthiest part of the court".

In the 18th century, this prestige of the court was challenged, particularly during the French Revolution, by the bourgeoisie (Father (l'abbé) Gregoire fought for the eradication of regional languages during the Revolution).

In the 19th century, it was up to the teacher training colleges (i.e Ecoles Normales) to train teachers, to transmit a standard relating to language but also to accents with pronunciation manuals.

In the 20th century, this norm was attributed to the Parisian bourgeoisie. In a concern for unification and following the social mixing between the two world wars, the pronunciation of the Parisian bourgeoisie spread to the middle classes, and quickly spread through the media.

Today, it is radio and television that define and convey the standard of pronunciation of a French called "standard".

The diffusion of an accepted and shared standard facilitates communication and exchange. But language is not only an instrument of communication, it is also a mirror of our identity. However, we seek to maintain (or safeguard) the reflexes of our ancestors by voluntarily or involuntarily maintaining our accent. The accent makes us unique, it allows us to define ourselves within a group, in connivance with people with whom we recognize enough common ground. Hence this force that

---

75 Au XVIe siècle, le grammairien anglais Jehan Palsgrave décrétait que la forme de français la plus pure était celle qui était parlée sur les bords de la Loire, en Touraine : « *Leur langage est le plus pur français, sans lenteur, sans vitesse, sans accent ; le berceau de la langue est là, près du berceau de la monarchie.* »
In the 16th century, the English grammarian Jehan Palsgrave decreed that the purest form of French was the one spoken on the banks of the Loire, in Touraine: "Their language is the purest French, without slowness, without speed, without accent; the cradle of the language is there, near the cradle of the monarchy. »

tends towards distinction, demarcation and identity affirmation. Our ancestors, when moving from one region to another, encountered these language differences and the fact that they had to make themselves understood and therefore attenuate or erase their accent. Returning to their country of origin, they had to do the opposite. All these mental actions are stressful.

The philosopher Jacques Derrida said that "The accent, and above all the strong southern accent, seemed to him incompatible with the dignity of a public word". Pierre Bourdieu, for his part, was ashamed of his Béarnais accent (a region close to the Pyrenees). On the other hand, an accent can be a "trademark" for artists, politicians or shopkeepers who want to promote local products; the southern accent, which evokes the sun and holidays, is at the top of this hierarchy. Marcel Pagnol is no stranger to this promotion. It is possible to have a career with this accent, while those in northeastern France have bad press (the "ch'ti" evokes greyness and the damaged steel industry) and can even discriminate against employment.

Less than a century ago, France was characterized by a mosaic of accents. For the last few decades, the time has come for homogenization. The accents tend to fade, to fade. In most varieties of French, the rolled "r" has been lost[76], the Parisian phonological system is essential. But the parochial spirit makes resistance in order to differentiate itself from the dominant society, or simply to rediscover a little of the conviviality that was probably idealized in the past. However, a Frenchman without an accent would be as sad as a village without a inhabitant.

Each region has its own coquetry of pronunciation that makes the regional accents so special. Some expressions are jealously guarded because they are picturesque, crispy and serve to preserve a small area of the language such as our secret garden that we share with a minority of people. They are precious assets because these regional parlours reflect a diversity within the French language in the same way as the accents that modulate its music. But not everything is rosy. However,

---

76 On l'entend encore un peu en Bresse bourguignonne ou dans l'Ariège

regional, social or foreign accents remain at the root of many discriminations, and just like language, accent makes it possible to integrate into a group but also to exclude.

In fact, the middle classes are abandoning these accents, which are considered incompatible with social advancement because the accent reveals a socio-demographic environment. The aim is to use a standardized French that makes it less and less possible to identify our origin, but this has not prevented the emergence of so-called social accents, thus delimiting sociocultural borders.

Factors of tension, stress, trauma, languages, patois, accents radiate around, swarm, enrich, enrich, insidiously leave their words. The problem comes from the context, from the times, not from words, not from sounds.

An accent is a legacy, the one left by men and women, by forgotten figures, crushed by the steamroller of history. An accent is what remains of the stories of the destinies of a group of human beings.

Chapter 9

The smells

There is another source of stress and transgenerational trauma that is quite underestimated, namely the loss of odours and their search over time.

Our ancestors lived surrounded by different smells than those around us. Each generation had its own scents. The one who left his farm to go to the city lost his olfactory references to gain other unwanted ones, imposed for which he was not prepared. City smells, factory smells, pollution smells. But despite this habituation, despite the time that erases the imprints, the memory of the past can reappear through smells as it reappears through sounds.

We are paying increasing attention to what we call a "better quality" environment and the place of "good smells" in our daily spaces, which raises the question of olfactory discomfort. This idea does not in fact correspond to any explicit reality, it does not have the status of a social problem and is not necessarily toxic. Our ancestors did not ask themselves these questions, smells were part of their environment. There were pleasant or unpleasant smells, but there were no "bad smells".

We all have smells that produce emotions without us knowing why. It is the smell of a damp room, the smell of the cellar, the garage, the attic where apples were stored, the smell of the Christmas tree that reminds us of our dreams and our childhood.

It is the smell of wood cooking, jam in summer, the smell of pies, roast on Sundays, the smell of lime blossom infusion in winter.

The smell of hay, of cut grass that was given to rabbits. The smell of the henhouse, the smell of wet dogs after the hunt.

It is the smell of fire that permeates our clothes. The older ones remembered the smell of ink at school, the smell of chalk and wet sponge.

There are also all the smells of nature, the smell of rain after a storm, the humidity of the woods, the smell of wild mint, the smell of dirt and dead leaves in the fall, the smell of mushrooms in the fall.

The birds singing at dawn corresponded to the particular smells of the morning.

There is the smell of incense in the church, candles and the church itself. The smell of the eaux de toilette of yesteryear.

It is also the smell of pond, manure in the courtyards of farms synonymous with rurality. The smell of wine and hot milk.

What could be the smells of yesteryear are nevertheless anchored in our memory and we are sensitive to them

Is there a form of genetic memory that is transmitted from one generation to the next? Some research[77] suggests that behaviours may be influenced by emotions felt in situations experienced by previous generations, and transmitted by what can be described as genetic memory.

However, it is difficult[78] to recover the perceptual systems of the past, with the values that underlie them. How can we access the understanding of a world that no longer exists by apprehending an element as furtive and subjective as sensitivity to the smells of our ancestors?

To be able to describe an image of the fragrant atmospheres of the past, we must question our olfactory sensitivity and the relationships we have with our urban and rural environments.

---

77 Dr Brian Dias et ses collègues de l'Université Emory : revue *Nature Neuroscience*

78 Alain Corbin dans ses recherches sur l'histoire du XIXe siècle

The geographical and historical spaces in which our ancestors lived were complex. The consultation of testimonies, health ordinances, regulations, municipal by-laws testifies to this. The words did not have the same meaning; what did "fetid emanation" mean, for example, except to describe that the streets were dirty, that there was a lack of hygiene, knowing that there was a great difference in sensitivity to odours between the urban and the peasant, or between the educated man and the less educated man. A banality for some, frightening olfactory images for others.

Leaving from the tranquility of their villages, peasants or emigrants such as masons, for example, found situations in the city that may have tested them hard; such as seeing fast and noisy carriages in often muddy streets, hearing the cries of street vendors, beggars, deafening noise, smelly smelling smells. They found themselves immersed in the brutal environment of an urban space delivered to the poorest social classes of which they were part. For centuries, cities were a challenge to hygiene. "The vices of the trippers and butchers, the skins of tanneries drying in the sun, the manure of horses and backyard animals, muddy streams, high humidity, narrow streets, cramped housing, insufficient sewers, piles of waste stored along the banks of rivers". These cities have assaulted the sense of smell of people in the countryside (and cities), increasing the already high stress due to their uprooting.

Some narratives give other testimonies: "Real centres of putrefaction, too small cemeteries overflow with their poorly buried corpses, the ditches of the enclosure fill with stagnant and foul-smelling water, especially in summer. In the middle of the roadway runs a gutter for rainwater drainage. Poorly maintained, it forms a distance apart from fetid cloacas, carrying waste water and garbage mixed with the bodies of small animals. The street, the stream, the ramparts commonly serve as public latrines and become the spillways of all rubbish, feeding goats, dogs, cats".

How could we not understand in these cases that so many diseases could have flourished? The air was pestilent. Everyone tried to perfume their clothes. "Fumigations of laurel, myrrh, camphor, pine, fir, spruce and larch were essential in the fight against the epidemic[79]. "Blankets, bed linen and tapestries were disinfected by burning under them juniper seed, putty, incense, Florence iris, storax, benzoin, tormentil and four to five handfuls of roses[80]. The profusion of these substances contributed to the olfactory intensity of the urban environment; people in the countryside were not prepared for all these irrational and unnatural smells.

Imagine for a moment that they could have been all these perfumes on a market day in villages and cities. Above the confusion and the noise, which must have been very intense, in a profusion of colours on more or less clean clothes, let us imagine these familiar fragrances of herbs, fruits, vegetables, flowers, cheeses, flour, grains, spices, candles, leathers.

These were all commodities that did not benefit farmers who were too poor for their own needs but had to sell them to survive.

But these people, our ancestors, loved to immerse themselves in this palette of smells that were sometimes aggressive and disgusting, sometimes sweet and honeyed. They must have been accustomed to the repulsive stench of blood, guts and fresh skins, especially if the butchers were trading in the streets, yards and squares covered with bones and rubbish. Our ancestors should not be inconvenienced by the incessant progress of the herds, by the screams of the slaughtered animals, by the stench of the waste.

They were probably sensitive to the smell of grilled meat when the sausage makers cooked sausages, bacon, hams and chops ready to eat on the spot with skinners selling offal, candle makers harvesting fat, tripe makers cooking viscera, while leatherers working on skins. All

---

79 Le Guérer 1984 : 58-69
80 Bordier 1896 : 70

these smells were familiar to them. It was only gradually that hygiene conditions became more severe.

Other mentalities took a long time to change, especially for certain industries. Thus, the textile and leather industries were driven by a fungal economy. For the craftsmen, "neither the sight nor the smell of excrement caused disgust". On the contrary, the visible accumulation of this garbage in front of their entrances meant prosperity and a greater likelihood of attracting the customer. Hence the widespread use of "urinal barrels" placed at the main intersections of the streets, intended to collect urine from passers-by and workers. In the evening, tanners, corroyers and scarves recovered the content for the practice of their art.

The dyer used putrefied urine mixed with vinegar to fix the colours of the fabrics and leathers. The scarves soaked their woven sheets in a wooden vessel filled with urine and warm soapy water to "remove the oil and other garbage that dirties them". In order for them to be penetrated and as if saturated, "bare legs and feet, they tread them with a heavy and regular step.[81]"

In the starch factory, whose workshop is immersed in particularly strong acid vapours, starch is produced by macerating wheat seeds in water until they germinate. He lets the mixture rest for a month, until the putrid decomposition takes hold of it. The washing, sieving and drying of the starch "then give rise to the abundant release of fetid fumes[82]".

The ragpicker collects and sorts all kinds of waste paper, rags, bones, skin and leather trimmings, which are recycled by the chemical and paper industries. All these materials, piled up in a jumble in a warehouse, facilitate the release of intolerable odours, dust and the presence of insects.

81 Ramazzini 1777 : 147
82 Monfalcon et de Polinière 1845 : 254

The most terrible smells are probably those that escape from craftsmen's workshops using the putrefaction of skins: candlesticks and skins.

Tanner[83], shrew and corker soften and facilitate the fall of hair and flesh remains from their dry skins by soaking them in tanks filled with lime water, arsenic and other ingredients. The skins, which smell terrible, are then washed with plenty of water and waxed. This operation requires extremely clear, sharp and cold water, free of factory waste water. Then the skins are put into "confit" in a fermented mixture of tan (oak bark reduced to flour).

These few examples paint a rather gloomy picture of people's living and working conditions, especially before the 18th century.

In any case, tasting the true pleasures of smell presupposes, for the enlightened mind of the Age of Enlightenment "Siècle des Lumières", a flight from the mud and manure, from the putrefaction of the bodies and confined spaces of the city: to join the "enchanting" countryside exalted by Rousseau and his disciples, which for them, stands out as a just space traversed by the breath of spring flowers. For some, the rich, the countryside is a sign of prosperity and wealth when in reality farmers are poor, sick, tired of hard work. The countryside is also a place of concentration of bad smells: the sweat of cattle, the droppings of poultry, the putrefaction of rat corpses, the accumulation of bodies living in a single room, the filth hidden in dark corners, the dust. The literary vision is idyllic, but the reality is morbid. The so-called "picturesque" journeys, fiction and iconography will contribute to distorting the true face of the countryside.

---

83 D'après le scientifique italien Ramazzini, qui, au XVIIIe siècle, s'est inquiété des maladies que subissent les artisans, « les corroyeurs, occupés à macérer les cuirs des animaux dans la chaux et la noix de galle, à les fouler aux pieds, à les laver, à les enduire de suif, sont attaqués par les exhalaisons sales et fétides qui s'élèvent des peaux. Ils ont le visage cadavéreux, ils sont enflés, d'une couleur livide.

According to the Italian scientist Ramazzini, who, in the 18th century, was concerned about the diseases suffered by craftsmen, "corroyers, who macerate animals' hides in lime and gall nuts, tread them down, wash them, coat them with tallow, are attacked by dirty exhalations and fetids that rise from the hides. They have a cadaverous face, they are swollen, of a livid color.

That said, it is important not to blacken the picture.

The discomfort caused by bad smells is a social problem that has lasted for several centuries. From the beginning of the 19th century, regulatory frameworks made it possible to reduce these odour nuisances by tackling the causes, and technical progress made it possible to reduce emissions that previously seemed unavoidable. Over the years, the regulations on this subject have become much richer.

Thus, for many centuries, the human world has been essentially fragrant. Then, suffocated under the domination of sight and hearing, smell became a secondary element. In recent years, odours have begun to reappear from oblivion and to conquer a dominant position as odours contribute to improving our way of life.

The members of the family tree studied shared many smells. The smells of the countryside, farms, animals are the olfactory foundations; then there will be the smells of workshops, transport, sweat smells, the smells of horses. Some will know the smells of powder, war, death. Others or the same ones will know the scents of the Saharan desert, the spices, the sea spray. The smells of diseases, hospitals, churches, will be shared by all.

These smells, some of them carriers of joy, have been the source of many traumas that will be transmitted from generation to generation.

Chapter 10

The memories

All the people in the family tree mentioned in the example dreamt and had memories. What could they be? Good or bad memories are inalienably linked to each person. These memories are part of ourselves and speak to us regularly.

These memories are in adequacy with a lifestyle; thus the memories of the one who lived in a village of Auvergne in the 17th century are different from the one who lived at the beginning of the 20th century.

We can also say that for each generation, our ancestors did not compensate their feelings of inferiority in the same way, did not position themselves in the same way towards the community or towards others, and staged themselves differently. Their anger, sulk, aggressiveness, indifference, or their relationship with seduction were also expressed differently. The perception that each generation of the past can be very different from reality and evolves with the change in our lifestyle.

During the vigils, memories were evoked, commented on, and passed from generation to generation. The stories thus conveyed were not necessarily those that had been lived but those that were remembered under the light of a distorting prism. A memory can be beautiful, rich, dramatic, moving; it always leaves a trace of its passage.

A memory has its own language, it does not speak the same way to the person who owns it or to the person who listens to it, proof that it has a very personal psychological environment.

What do we know about the childhood memories of our ancestors? It is likely that traces of tragic events can be found there and that the affection was absent.

How many lives in one have our forefathers counted? The house and village of their birth, their life as young men and women, their marriage, their parents' situation. Lives at school, religious education, travel or migration, the army, changes in occupations have complicated their lives. Some had a small number, especially before the 18th century, others had many lives.

If we refer to the stories of the members of this family tree, happiness is not related to the importance of the number of lives.

Each of these lives hides a little bit of richness that can be found in memories. These are the invisible bonds that weave our personality. Memories are our personal signature, a proof that we have lived.

When these memories are not passed on, through the premature death of the father or mother, a void forms for subsequent generations.

In the family tree used as an example, people died quite early. This loss of memory has resulted in a loss of family memory.

We will not know anything about their secrets, their loves, their pains and their sorrows.

Our memories are the links in a chain as important as DNA.

Our memories are for us a wonderful space of freedom, a private space where no one can enter or control without our agreement. We are the masters of our stories, our fantasies and our lies. Memories are the only things that cannot be stolen from us.

It seems that the people in this family tree had only their memories as property, which they did not wish to share.

The lives of our ancestors were wrapped in memories, it was their inner skin. But we know neither this one nor their carnal envelope, in fact we do not know them and we try to know them by attempts to analyze them from dates, names, situations with the risk of making mistakes.

However, a smell, an image, a sound, a place, can revive in us a memory that does not necessarily belong to us. We are flirting here with the limits of the unconscious.

For a long time immaterial, we are increasingly seeking to preserve memories in the form of trinkets, decorated plates, statuettes, postcards, photos, films, but each of these supports remains surrounded by a halo that we are the only ones to see.

Only a few decades ago, the interior of houses was very bare, especially for farmers' and workers' houses.

Where did the material form of the memories nestle? In the characteristic of the hooves, the walking stick that was carved, in the dishes, in the embroidery of the sheets, in the grandfather's hat, the worn pipe, in the annotated missal filled with pious images and many other very humble and very simple traces. All these memories could disappear at the same time as the deceased by putting them in his coffin.

Today we are collecting a lot of souvenirs that will one day go to a garage sale. In these places where war crosses are bought, a simple preformed metal object stripped of all that has made the glory of the one who owned it and that we will never know. The object loses all its real value when it loses its emotional charge.

What were the relics, fetishes, treasures of the people of this family tree? We don't know that. Their graves, other places of memory have also disappeared.

Even if our ancestors had left us memories, they would have done as we did, that is, they would probably have selected them, forgetting those who did not suit them or disturbed them. Would they have been better accountants for their memories? Probably yes because we have become too scrupulous because our close love is now trying to dominate our memory. It also seems that we have developed the ability to make screen memories in such a way as to hide memories that we do not want to see appear. But it's a lost cause; a hidden or forgotten memory will one day come back on its own.

A baby probably has the ability to store memories during intrauterine life around five months of pregnancy. It is safe to think that he feels a lot of things and that his feelings are accumulating. At birth the first look is important, as is the first carnal contact. Let us now go back to the past, we see that the lives of babies were very different from those of today's babies. Pregnant, the women worked in the fields, on farms or later in the factory. The baby's relationships with his future father and then his father were reduced if not absent. Father-mother-child nuclearity was very different from generation to generation. Tenderness and complicity were very often absent in favour of rigour and severity.

We saw that the parents in this family tree died quite early. The role of the extended family (uncle, aunt, cousin, nephew,...) was therefore important. The relational balance and social feeling that these children were able to develop in relation to others were therefore different. If memories make it possible to stabilize emotional states, we can then question the influence that these situations have had on their psychological resources and the traumas they have caused.

From the age of three or five, the child is strongly influenced by the parents' lifestyle, by his or her relationships with his or her father and mother, by his or her place in the siblings or in the family constellation. Very early on, therefore, it forges his personality, and he very early develops his own lifestyle that he can keep all his life and transmit to his descendants. However, since nothing is decided definitively, and since the mistakes of the journey can be repaired or compensated for over time and depending on the situation, the prototype of adult life can be very different from the prototype of childhood life. From a hereditary soil come individual, family and social experiences; this pathway can be positive but also fraught with pitfalls.

Consider a criterion such as Self-esteem "estime de Soi"[84]. The child needs internal and external security, an identity base so that he or

84 Définition de la National Associationfor Self Esteem- www2.csmb.qc.ca/estimedesoi

she recognizes himself or herself as a unique and different being, a sense of belonging to a community, and can give meaning to his or her life. From this comes a sense of competence that allows him to define challenges that are right for him.

How do the characters in the family tree define themselves on these five criteria?

Gervais (1766-1809) was born from a third marriage and was 14 years old at the death of his father Marien (1723-1780), he was an only child but close to his cousins. He stayed on his lands in Auvergne. The extended family seemed pretty tight-knit. Owner it had to correspond favorable to the feeling of self-esteem "Estime de Soi".

Annet (1793-1862) son of Gervais (above) was the 3rd child out of 5, 6 years older than the eldest. He was 8 years old when his mother died and 16 years old when his father died[85]. Declared as a farmer, his sense of self-esteem may not have been very positive even though the sense of belonging to a community (extended family and family with 8 children) may have been strong. Married at 32 years old and therefore quite late for unknown reasons, unless he has done years in the army, his children will become masons. His wife was fatherless at his marriage. If his need for security was ensured within a community, it does not seem that he was able to develop his potential skills.

Mathieu (1834-1898) son of Annet above, was 28 years old when his father died and 26 years old when his mother died. He was the third of the siblings. He left his native region young enough to settle in Beaujolais. He married Jeanne, her father's orphan, at the age of 25. His internal and external security had disappeared when he left. He didn't join a group. He was unable to develop his potential skills. Of his 7 children, five died before the age of 6. The conditions are not there to have good self-esteem.

Jean-Marie (1859-1905), Mathieu's eldest son. He was 39 years old when his father died and 32 years old when his mother died. At the age

---

85 On notera que plus tard Lucien (1924) avait 16 ans à la mort de son père Louis-Antoine (1894-1940) et 9 ans à la mort de sa mère Jeanne (1896-1933)

of 24, he married Benoite, from a not very wealthy family. Mason, he will have 8 children, with the feeling of creating a family community that does not exist. Its identity base must have been fragile. He was unable to develop his potential skills. He died at 45 for an unknown reason. The conditions are not in place for him to have a good self-esteem.

Antoine, son of Jean-Marie and number two of the siblings was also a mason. He was 19 years old when his father and breadwinner died. He didn't know or could give meaning to his life. Quite socially destabilized, he died in 1919 just after the return of the First World War. Her self-esteem was pretty low. He had to deal with a number of family torments.

Jeanne, Jean-Marie's daughter, and number three in the siblings, married at the age of 18 in the same year as the year her father died. She died of illness five years after having had a natural son, Henri, at the age of 20. The conditions for good self-esteem are clearly not in place. When she married at 18, she needed security, but she didn't. The birth of a child could have given her a meaning to her life, but she abandoned her son. The disease may be responsible for this failure.

Jacques, Jean-Marie's second son and the 4th child of the siblings, was 14 years old when his father died. At the age of 18, he joined the army for economic reasons or to join a stable community. Back from the war, he married and did several jobs in Lyon before returning to Beaujeu. He could not or did not express his potential skills. His only son, too, will not have the opportunity to have a good self-esteem. He will die of an accident at 57 years of age, without means, after having divorced.

Louis-Antoine is Jean-Marie's 3rd son and the 5th child of the siblings. He was 11 years old when his father died. His childhood up to this age could have been happy if we refer to the time and conditions of his social class. His education is good. But as soon as her father dies, a number of events occur within her family and within her mother's family. He joined the army like his brother Jacques at the age of 18. He thus joins a community. His various military assignments, his acts of war are as many challenges as he comes back alive. He tries to give meaning to his life by going back to the gendarmerie school, becoming a mounted gendarme, and a blacksmith. A son will be born from his union with Jeanne.

But she died 11 years later of illness. So he had several very different lives. But he could not recall his memories or even leave them to his son because, remembering in 1938, he died in 1940. Did he have good self-esteem? After all these trials, words give meaning to one's life and take on many values. His life has been more like an obstacle course.

His son Lucien, who returned to the Ecole de la Marine at the age of 16, after his father's death. He will join a stable community here. His paternal and maternal families were reduced to only a few people with whom he could keep some semblance of contact. He married Colette, the eldest daughter of a large and relatively wealthy family, at the age of 25. A sense of self-esteem is positive and will also positively dictate the lives of one's children.

We have followed here some members of a family name, we could study the life of wives in the same way. It is not a confidence to say that their lives are no different from those of their respective husbands and that they may face considerable challenges given the unfavourable social conditions.

We are far from evoking an emotional memory like the first kiss... it is hard to imagine.

It is our emotional perception of things, in accordance with the personality we have built up over the years, our successes and failures, that will cause something to be felt as futile or striking. Thus the index of values of things perceived by Louis-Antoine, a military man, was certainly very different from the index of values of his grandfather Gervais in the 18th century.

Let's try to imagine what memories the above-mentioned people may have had :

Gervais (1766-1809), from a third marriage, only child, had as memories the life of the farm, the scents, and the early work.

Annet (1793-1862) son of Gervais (above), 3rd child out of 5, 6 years older than the eldest. He was 8 years old when his mother died. He may have felt a little lonely and devoid of affection.

Mathieu (1834-1898) son of Annet above. Third of the siblings. His memories probably include his long hoof trips to school and the cold weather in the classroom.

Jean-Marie (1859-1905), Mathieu's eldest son. He liked to play on the small bridge in the lively Pont Paradis de Beaujeu district, near the tannery factory.

Antoine, son of Jean-Marie and number two of the siblings (his older sister died at the age of 2) probably accompanied his father to the construction sites very early on. His childhood dreams could be dreams of escape.

Jeanne, Jean-Marie's daughter, and number three in the family, played with her cousins and dreamed of getting out of her neighbourhood, from the polluting atmosphere of the nearby factory.

Jacques, Jean-Marie's second son and the 4th child of the siblings, was divided between his father's work and the duty to go to school.

Louis-Antoine, Jean-Marie's 3rd son and 5th child of the siblings, had gained in freedom, he dreamed of travelling and his memories could be walks in the nearby woods. By becoming a rider in the 10th Cuirassiers Regiment, caring for a horse is perhaps a real value of an emotional compensation due to loneliness, grief and illness. We are not far from this truth.

Lucien, son of Louis-Antoine, will remember his father's horse, his long walks to see his uncles and to go to school.

...These are only plausible assumptions.

It seems that there is a common denominator, it is the dream of escape, an opening towards the outside world perhaps linked to a feeling of solitude.

Some childhood years are covered with a layer of mystery. The word 'childhood'[33] itself calls for a set of particular sensations based on our senses, sensations, emotions, feelings and emotional thoughts.

If we could ask the above-mentioned people to describe their childhood memories, it is almost certain that these memories would be unspontaneous and filtered by their current concerns and would appear in a confusing disorder.

On the other hand, for most of them, memories would invoke displacement or travel, voluntary or sudden. With regard to their respective lives, it was oriented towards the outside world. The security and warmth of a house does not seem to have been a major factor. This notion of displacement is symbolized by the trades of mason, soldier, horse, and moving. This need for travel has increased over generations up to now.

The people presented in this tree have suffered many traumas, sufferings, miseries, injustices, abandonments. We now know that our bodies are somatized, with migraines, muscle aches, stomach aches and various diseases, it is not inconceivable to think that these people had a number of these worries. Early mortality, the diseases that took them away can be a consequence of these traumas, a set of emotional tensions could predispose a person to get a disease. Reference will be made to the explanations of child psychiatrist Marcel Rufo saying that "the symptom is never there by chance, it is always attached to an internal psychological event or an external traumatic event". It does not always work of course because we are always able to overcome a painful event with the nuance advanced by Boris Cyrulnik "a blow hurts, but it is the representation of the blow that makes the trauma".

But all these people died without being able to express themselves, we can only let our imagination run free to judge the importance of their traumas and their causes but without compassion, without feeling sorry for themselves and without affecting each other.

Remembrance and oblivion are part of the process of our memory, it is up to us to sort it out, our forefathers have the right to keep their shares of mystery.

. . . The word END does not appear on our page

Realizing your family tree is a moving and exciting investigation and exploration project.

This research allows, through the discovery of one's family history, to reach a better knowledge of oneself, of one's strengths, and to explain one's weaknesses or at least the probable origin of them.

A family tree is in fact the sum of a series of investigations from which revelations, unspoken words, ghosts emerge, but also from which the tasks of suffering, illness and misery emerge. Going back over the painful past of some of our ancestors is delicate, it is necessary to proceed with a certain hindsight in order not to affect each other.

The analysis of our most distant memories can be a good starting point because this analysis is a way to look behind the mirror for explanations about the facts and mechanisms that have made us who we are. The knowledge of our forefathers already requires a better knowledge of ourselves. Nothing that is done in us, nothing that happens to us happens by chance, everything makes sense. Our conscious and unconscious minds constantly intervene to remind us of this, but we do not know how to listen to them or rather decipher this information. Our memories must not be the poor parents of our psychic life, quite the contrary, they are the immaterial link that connects us to those who were there before us and to whom we succeed.

A family novel is complicated, full of mysteries that we seek to shed light on, cluttered with lost cases that we seek to justify and rehabilitate. We run into many locked doors that will not open even if all the bells have been pulled.

In our minds, we must order a method based on the dates, first names, jobs carried out, a certain number of decodings. It is necessary to make connections, sorting, juxtapositions, concordances, concomitances. We must follow leads, discover secrets, do not judge, we must protect ourselves from the poisons of the past.

This decoding thus gradually becomes meaningful.

We carry family memories that are part of the great history and in a certain socio-cultural context. We are not obliged to understand, but above all we must protect ourselves from both grief and shame. Emotions are still distilled in us, but we now have the burdens of the generations that we can deposit, thus gaining our freedom, but this action is not easy to achieve.

This decoding thus gradually becomes meaningful.

We carry family memories that are part of the great history and in a certain socio-cultural context. We are not obliged to understand, but above all we must protect ourselves from both grief and shame. Emotions are still distilled in us, but we now have the burdens of the generations that we can deposit, thus gaining our freedom, but this action is not easy to achieve.

In every time period crossed there are family tragedies and disorders that have consequences on the following generations. The resulting trauma may be resolved through external action or other trauma.

We bear the mark of our environment; we are imbued with what constitutes the habits and customs of our region of birth and its traditions, its history, the atmosphere of the social and cultural environment in which we grew up. All this baggage is increased by the many imprints of the environments in which our ancestors evolved, rooted themselves in all these events.

These local, regional, historical facts infiltrate us from birth from deep and numerous roots; memories of tragedies and injustice shake in us without us perceiving it. But all these movements are present.

The social and cultural background of our ancestors was not the same as that of our childhood. Many of these families lived in what would now be called "economic difficulties", the notion of a poverty line did not exist at the time, and our ancestors took a long time to reach a more enviable social level.

The descendants may or may not have assimilated this social evolution, but there is very often an unconscious feeling of disloyalty for having overcome the social status of the origins. Some families set themselves a social status that should not be exceeded, as is often the case for workers, craftsmen and traders, and this situation can lead to a fairly frequent class neurosis for anyone who wants to examine this phenomenon. This prohibition corresponds to parental injunctions which most of the time are not clearly stated but smoulder in the ashes of words intended to discourage certain initiatives. For example, an allusion to the evil our ancestors had to do to earn a living can be a barrier to progress and the desire for enrichment.

There are many prohibitions everywhere, even in dates, diseases, secrets.

Prohibitions and attitudes are the links in an unbroken chain. To free oneself from this chain, one must know, understand and choose. Freedom is at the end of this process.

Our ancestors come to us with their luggage, but we are not obliged to carry it.

Bibliography

[1] Broch H., (1985), Le paranormal, Seuil.

[2] Canault N. (1998), Comment paye-t-on les fautes de ses ancêtres ? , Desclée De Brouwer.

[3] Jean Cottraux, (2001), La répétition des scénarios de vie, Odile Jacob

[4] Patrice Van Eersel, Catherine Maillard, (2002), J'ai mal à mes ancêtres, Albin Michel

[5] Ancelin Schützenberger A., (2000), Aie, mes aieux ! , 15e édition, Desclée De Brouwer.

[6] Ancelin Schützenberger A., (2011), Exercices pratiques de psychogénéalogie, Petite bibliothèque Payot

[7] Hilgard J. R (1953), Anniversary reactions in Parents precipitated by Children, Psychiatry, 16, pp. 73-80.

[8] Hilgard J.R., Newman M. (1961), Evidence for functional genesis in mental Illness : Schizophrenia, depressive psychoses and psychoneuroses, J. Nerv. Mental. Dis., pp. 11-13.

[9] Géraldine Favre, Les dossiers de l'OZ

[10] Alexandre Jollien, (2006), La construction de soi, Editions du Seuil

[11] Boris Cyrulnik, (2006) , De chair et d'Âmes, Odile Jacob

[12] Nietzsche, (1985), La généalogie de la morale, Gallimard

[13] Paul Watzlawick, (1980), Le langage du changement, Editions du seuil

[14] Jacques Lecomte, (2007) Donner un sens à sa vie, Odile Jacob

[15] David Eagleman, (2013), Incognito, les vies secrètes du cerveau R Laffont

[16] C.G.Jung, (1964), Dialectique du Moi et de l'inconscient, Gallimard

[17] C.G.Jung, (1963), L'Âme et la vie, Editions Buchet/Chastel

[18] C.G.Jung, (1973), L'énergétique psychique, Georg éditeur

[19] Pierre Daco, Les prodigieuses victoires de la psychologie, Marabout

[20] Eugen Weber, (1983), La fin des terroirs, la modernisation de la France 1870-1914, Librairie A. Fayard

[21] Bruno Bettelheim (1976): Psychanalyse des contes de fée, R. Laffont

[22] Ivan Boszormenui-Nagy (1973), Invisible Loyalties, Reciprocity in Intergenerational Family Therapy, Harper &Row

[23] J. Semonsous (1938), « Pages d'histoire- Basse Auvergne »

[24] Danielle Nicouleau, 2004, Etre sans ses ancêtres, Presses du midi

[25] Gustave-Nicolas Fisher, 1997, La psychologie sociale, Ed. Seuil

[26] L.Tatu, J.Bogousslavsky, 2012, La folie au front, Ed. Imago

[27] Antoine Sylvère- La rudesse d'une enfance paysanne

[28] Michel Ragon- La ferme d'en haut

[29] Michel Ragon- Le cocher du Boiroux

[30] Jean-Louis Magnon- Blanche de solitude

[31] Emmanuel Le Roy Ladurie-
Le paysan français de l'Ancien Régime, du XIXème au XVIIIème siècle.

[32] Luce Janin-Devillard- Ces morts qui vivent en nous- Fayard

[33] Patrick Estrade- Ces souvenirs qui nous gouvernent- Robert Laffont

[34] Frédéric Lenoir- Les métamorphoses de Dieu-Plon 2003

[35] Paul Ricoeur – La mémoire, l'histoire, l'oubli- Le Seuil 2003

[36] Jean-Pierre Changeux – L'homme de vérité- Odile Jacob

[37] Paul Perrève – La Burle, un médecin de campagne en Haute-Ardèche- JC Lattès

[38] Henri Vincenot- La billebaude- Denoel

[39] Alfred Adler- Le sens de la vie – Payot

[40] Alfred Adler-la psychologie de la vie – L'Harmattan

[41] Siri Hustvedt- Vivre Penser Regarder- Actes Sud

Internet links

On psychogenealogy:

http://www.psychogenealogie.com
http://www.psychologies.com/cfml/toutsurlestherapies/
http://www.geneapsy.com
School of training in psychogenealogy and transgenerational analysis

Anne Ancelin Schützenberger's website:
http://perso.wanadoo.fr/a.ancelin.schutzenberger/

Birthday syndrome:
http://www.retrouversonnord.be/syndrAnniv.htm

Warning:

http://www.prevensectes.com/psy1.htm#22
http://www.francefms.com
http://www.psyvig.com

Appendices

Curvilinear Component Analysis

The discovery of small varieties in large data is one of the objectives of learning methods and data topology techniques.

In the book "Méthodes de visualisation de données à fortes dimensions dans un espace réduit à 2 D" by C-A Saby, in reading on https://fr.calameo.com/books/0004584722c9f8be8cdf4

are particularly studied linear and non-linear methods of dimensionality reduction in the context of data visualization. A number of concrete examples are presented, some original uses of these methods have been patented. This common framework includes traditional methods such as Principal Component Analysis (PCA), Independent Component Analysis (ICA) and Multidimensional Scaling (MDS) that are considered good for data manipulation and are inherently linear in nature.

Non-linear techniques such as curvilinear component analysis (CCA), Sammon's map, "Locally Linear Embedding" (LLE), "Hesse LLE" (HLLE), "Kernel PCA", "relational perspective map" (RPM), Isomap, "Isotope Method", Kohonen's map, "Generative Topographic Mapping" (GTM) can operate effectively on non-linear data. However, these algorithms unfold the data space in a different way so that their performance depends on the type and structure of the data to be analyzed. In the experiments presented, the most powerful algorithms for these data, which cover both real and artificial situations, were CCA and Sammon.

Both techniques (PCA and ICA) assume a linear model of the data structure, but in the general case of a non-linear model, they do not provide any information.

The Curvilinear Component Analysis algorithm, or CCA, makes it possible to avoid linearity assumptions and to process a wide variety of data structures. The simplicity of the calculations it involves and its convergence mode make it easier to use than other more traditional "non-linear" algorithms.

This algorithm is a powerful tool for determining the intrinsic dimension of a variety representing a data structure. The method provides a good" estimate of the number of free parameters on which the data structure depends.

The principle is simple: it is a matter of mapping the data space with a small space. First, a vector quantification of the data space is performed by a number N of prototypes x_i, then the y_i images of these prototypes are searched in the projection space by locally copying their distances two by two.

Reminders of some definitions

Psychology is the science that studies mental behaviours and processes and the applications that can be made of acquired knowledge. The vocation of psychology is twofold: to accumulate theoretical knowledge, but also to provide support to people with psychological functioning problems.

Sociology, derived from the human sciences such as psychology, is the science that studies particular social facts and behaviours or considered as a whole.

The human sciences have created spaces for encounters around human facts that require a multidisciplinary approach for their understanding.

Anthropology is the science that studies the human being in his physical evolution, but also through his social and cultural activities.

Cognitive sciences has been a new sector for about 25 years, bringing together many disciplines in the exact and experimental sciences around disciplines in the human sciences. There are disciplines such as psychology, linguistics, philosophy, anthropology, artificial intelligence, neuroscience, etc... grouped around the same project, the study of knowledge activity in all its forms: perception, memory, language, learning, problem solving, conceptualization (thinking), planning of passionate behaviours, emotion management, action.

The cognitive sciences assume that the organism is a system that acts intelligently in its environment, making it a mental representation that it constantly adapts to its needs and beliefs.

"Psychology has been enriched by neuroscience discoveries about how the brain functions and how it relates to behaviour. Understanding who we are is based first and foremost on understanding the biological roots of behaviour both in terms of our genetic heritage and in terms of the functioning of our bodies and, more specifically, our brains.

The ever-increasing knowledge of brain chemistry tells us that the substances secreted by the brain are responsible for triggering and directing nerve messages. It is, in particular, through the action of these substances that emotions, stress, hunger, dreams etc. come to us... The existence of the human being consists in a constant interaction with the surrounding world allowing the individual to ensure his adaptation and, by extension, his survival from birth to death. At any given moment, human beings are confronted with situations whose importance varies according to their needs or objectives.

Western psychophysiology recognizes 2 states of consciousness specific to all individuals: sleep, considered as a rest period, and the state of alertness or active vigilance. The latter state corresponds to an activation of the entire organism that allows it to capture, select and process information from the outside world, to keep some in memory or to react to others with appropriate or inappropriate behaviours, depending on previous experiences or learning. The state of awakening is therefore that of adaptation to external reality.

Ordinary consciousness is the normal state that essentially translates into the ability to decode and respond effectively to environmental stimuli. The way we become aware of both our inner and outer world is largely "imbued" with the cultural habits of the social group with which we identify. It changes over time, with age, and also on a daily basis.

The decoding of events will be very different depending on whether you are relaxed or anxious, excited or near sleep, young and inexperienced or old.
»

A family tree is the perception of a vertical world. When you do it, you go for a walk in another world, you walk freely, you observe without judging, but you don't come back unscathed.

Our unconscious has long since been colonized.

This document attempts to determine the influence that our ancestors had on us, our behaviour and our way of life.

Based on a concrete example of an Auvergne family over seven generations, we will study here the extent of the various traumas these people have suffered and the consequences on their descendants.

ISBN 978-0-244-49239-7

90000

9 780244 492397